Hum

MW01120824

Featuring

Travels with Fred,
the World's Worst Tourist

Praise for
Bruce Gravel's first novel:

Inn-Sanity:
Diary of an Innkeeper Virgin

"The book is PRICELESS!! In fact, I read it twice!"
– Mark Covey, owner/operator, Howard Johnson Tillsonburg

"Being in the motel business, I always look for books on hospitality. Unfortunately, good ones are rare. I found this book to be everything I was looking for. FUNNY, EASY TO READ and oh, so true. VERY RECOMMENDED! It will put a smile on your face."
– C.B. Zucker, posting a **5 Star** review on Amazon.com

"GREAT COTTAGE READING! I certainly could relate to it."
– Nick Vesely, General Manager,
The Sutton Place Hotel, Toronto

"I THOROUGHLY ENJOYED IT. So close to reality! The pages kept turning. Great characters throughout. However, THE ENDING SCARED THE DAYLIGHTS OUT OF ME!"
– Pam Fischer, owner/operator, Lake Edge Cottages, Lakefield

"Being in the hotel industry, I found this to be A GREAT READ. I think EVERYONE WILL ENJOY THIS BOOK, as it gives a window into the very funny situations we encounter, working at hotels for a living."
– Paul Moran, General Manager, Howard Johnson
Toronto-Markham, posting a **5 Star** review on Amazon.com

Praise for
Bruce Gravel's first short story collection:

Humour on Wry, with Mustard

To Dana, Paul & Maren —

Humour on Wry, with Mayo

Featuring

Enjoy!
Bruce
Gravel.

TRAVELS WITH FRED, THE WORLD'S WORST TOURIST

Bruce Gravel

Illustrations by Bob Sherwood

Wigglesworth & Quinn
Peterborough

Humour on Wry, with Mayo
featuring
Travels with Fred, the World's Worst Tourist

For information, contact: bruce@brucegravel.ca.

Published by: Wigglesworth & Quinn, Peterborough, Ontario, Canada
Ordering Information: bruce@brucegravel.ca
Printed in the United States of America

First Edition: November 2010

Library and Archives Canada Cataloguing in Publication

Gravel, Bruce M. (Bruce Magnus), 1952 -
    Humour on wry, with mayo featuring travels with Fred, the world's worst tourist / Bruce Gravel ; illustrations by Bob Sherwood.

ISBN 978-1-4538-4936-1

    1.   Canadian wit and humor (English).
2.   Travel--Humor.   I. Title.

PS8613.R369H84 2010   C818'.602   C2010-906910-2

Everything is better with Mayo too.

Dedication

To Frances and Scott,
for their wonderful inspiration and honest feedback,
and for relentlessly pressuring me to finish this book,
under the guise of love and encouragement.

And for continuing to believe in me
despite all evidence to the contrary.

(There: That's three books published in
three years. May I be unshackled now? Please?)

Author's Note

In Book One, *Travels with Fred*, the characters of Fred, the World's Worst Tourist, and Rachel, his long-suffering wife, are entirely fictional, bearing no resemblance to anyone living, dead, or half-dead. However, **most of the incidents that happen to, or are caused by, Fred are based on true events**.

Anyone who has travelled, or who, like innkeepers and airline crew, caters to travellers, has encountered people like Fred. People like Fred give the exhilarating, fulfilling, and pleasurable experience of travel a bad name, inhibiting the exhilaration, poking holes in the fulfillment, and throwing cold water on the pleasure. Thankfully, people like Fred are few and far between. But they *are* out there. Dammit.

Bruce Gravel
Peterborough, Ontario
October 2010

Acknowledgements

My grateful thanks and appreciation go to the people who related the true travel incidents that provided grist for some of my *Travels with Fred* mill, including Pam Fischer, Joe Hetherton, Ted Fotiadis, Richard Lafleur, Lynda Cunningham, and especially Frances and Scott Gravel.

May your luggage never be lost.

In Book Two, *Humour on Wry, with Mayo*, my equally-grateful thanks and appreciation go to the folks who provided incidents (some of them **true**) and/or inspiration that formed the basis for some of my allegedly-funny tales, including Dave and Shamim Warren, John Gravel, Lucinda and Mike St. Pierre, Pat and Connie Slinn, Sue Maskell, Maxine Slanic, Lynda Cunningham, and again especially Frances and Scott Gravel.

May your smiles always be warm.

The covers and interior illustrations were done by Bob Sherwood, a professional caricaturist living in Ontario. Contact Cartoon Bob at: 905-659-5498. Email: cartoonbob@cogeco.ca.

Shorter versions of a few of these stories previously appeared in the *Peterborough Examiner* newspaper between June 2008 and June 2009.

"Conventional Wisdom meets Unconventional Reality" previously appeared in *Association* magazine, April/May, 2007.

Shorter versions of several stories previously appeared in *The Accommodator* magazine between February, 2009, and October, 2010.

Huge thanks to Frances Gravel for her great job in the formatting and lay-out of the entire book, getting it all print-ready. Many thanks to Scott Gravel for conceptualizing and designing the covers, and electronically enabling the printing of this book by means of arcane voodoo.

What a wonderful family affair!

Book One: Chapters

TRAVELS WITH FRED, THE WORLD'S WORST TOURIST

Book Two: Chapter 5
Humour on Wry, with Mayo

Book One:

TRAVELS WITH FRED, THE WORLD'S WORST TOURIST

Vive le Fred Libre!

Fred and Rachel's Montreal Getaway

Fred, poster boy for The Tourist From Hell, accompanied his wife, Rachel, on a weekend getaway to Montreal. Their escape-from-Toronto furlough had two objectives: romantic canoodling without business distractions and some live theatre.

They were both disappointed: Rachel with the quality and quantity of the canoodling, and Fred upon discovering that "live theatre" was Rachel-speak for opera, which he enjoyed as much as a root canal.

What an unlikely couple was what folks usually thought when they first saw Fred and Rachel. She was a petite, energetic woman just over five feet tall, with flashing blue eyes and black hair cropped short in a severe angular style. Her pleasing figure was always one buffet away from plump, and she exuded a focused, businesslike attitude.

In contrast, Fred was over six feet tall, gangly, with extraordinarily-long spindly legs and very large feet. His hair, muddy brown in colour and starting to thin, was composed of long wispy tendrils that wafted about in the slightest breeze, as if possessed of a life of their own and eager to escape their owner. His long, narrow face had a slightly-vacant, somewhat inquisitive expression, like that of a squirrel wondering just where it buried those damned nuts. The squirrel resemblance was abetted by wide buck teeth that protruded slightly from his mouth.

When they stood together, Rachel barely came up to Fred's bony chest. They were also polar opposites in temperament; she being optimistic and he being a walking gloom cloud.

On their last night in their swank hotel, in a city famous for its French cuisine, Fred surprised Rachel with a sumptuous classy dinner from room service (the pizza came with three extra toppings and fancy paper napkins), followed by an in-room "chick flick" selected by Rachel (which Fred fell asleep in the middle of).

Around midnight, Fred awoke to a dark room and a snoring spouse. Naked (his preferred sleeping attire), he fumbled out of bed to visit the bathroom and stepped in the tray with the remains of dinner, whereupon "there arose such a clatter."

Rachel snored on. Years of listening to Fred's sonorous pontificating meant she could sleep through a five-alarm fire.

Fred flicked on the bathroom light and picked up the tray to banish it outside their room.

First, he prudently looked through the door's peephole, to check if the coast was clear. No one. He opened the door and stuck his head out, looking up and down the corridor. Empty.

Reassured, he stepped out and placed the tray down on the hall carpet as the door closed behind him.

Fred straightened, pirouetted, and turned the door handle. The door didn't open. After several more attempts, he realized this was a self-locking door, considerately installed by hotel management to ensure guest security, so weird undesirables couldn't get in.

Resplendent in his birthday suit, Fred now qualified as a weird undesirable.

Knowing it was utterly futile, yet having no other options, Fred tapped on the door, to awaken Rachel.

His tapping escalated to knocking, then pounding, then pounding with yelling.

A man's head popped out, several rooms away. His angry scowl morphed into astonishment upon seeing Fred *au naturel*. The head disappeared and the door clicked shut.

Desperate, Fred scooted up to the head's door and shouted through it, asking the man to please call the front desk to send someone up with a master key.

Further down the hall, another door opened. A sweet grandmotherly face emerged, framed by a briar patch of gigantic curlers. She gawked at the naked pervert who had disturbed her sleep, then unleashed a fusillade of choice words in both official languages that would be quite at home in a logging camp. The pinko sicko galumphed towards her, eyes pleading, begging her to let him inside. She slammed the door in his face.

The elevator dinged. More people! Aghast, Fred fled to the other end of the long hall and flung himself through the door leading to the stairwell.

En route, he provided quite a show as he streaked past peepholes now filled with curious eyes.

A burly security guard discovered Fred cowering inside the stairwell door, covered in nothing but goosebumps.

With the guard's cap concealing his intimates, Fred slunk back to his door, which the guard opened with his master keycard. Rachel was still sawing wood.

Checking out next morning, Rachel wondered why the front desk clerks were sniggering.

She heard raucous laughter through the open door of the nearby security office. The staff were watching something on a monitor, and though her French was rusty, she understood it was quite funny.

So funny, that multiple copies were being requested.

Innkeepers have told your author that hotel security cameras capture some amazing things, from nude and semi-nude guests in hallways, to nookie in deserted swimming pools and spas. I now regret some of my youthful indiscretions.

Fred Handles an Emergency

Not because he paid extra for it, because Fred didn't believe in paying extra for anything, but because the seat was unsold and the flight attendant took pity on Fred's long spindly legs crammed into a regular seat space. So that's how Fred, the World's Worst Tourist, found himself ensconced in the roomier Emergency Exit aisle, right next to the Emergency Exit door.

Rachel, miffed because her petite legs kept her in a regular seat, thought the flight attendant deserved whatever she got by putting Fred in a position of responsibility. Then she thought of how pleasant the flight would be without her perpetually-complaining husband next to her for five hours, and a feeling of goodwill towards flight attendants suffused her.

As the final passengers fumbled towards their seats and the plane prepared to depart, the flight attendant instructed Fred and his two seatmates in the Emergency Exit row, about their required actions should an emergency transpire. It involved lifting a big handle on the Emergency door and pushing it open.

Three bobbleheads all nodded their understanding.

The flight attendant moved away, not knowing that Fred had a big problem with instructions. For example, when briefed on the new ultra-security procedures to access the restricted area at the government agency that had the misfortune of employing him, Fred misunderstood the retinal scan instructions. He caused quite an incident when he approached the wall-mounted scanner for the first time, turned, dropped his trousers, and presented his bare backside to the device.

He thought they said rectal scan. Two file clerks, who had been standing nearby, are still in therapy, at taxpayers' expense.

As the plane door closed and the powerful engines spooled up, Fred stared at the Emergency door that had been placed in his care. He wondered how often the release mechanism was tested, to verify that it operated the way it should.

He consoled himself that it was probably tested on a regular basis. But still ...

Exactly how frequently? And was the tester competent, or careless because of years of repetitive testing?

The plane was pushed back from the terminal.

In a real emergency, it would be catastrophic if the door didn't open. Many would die. Especially him.

So wouldn't he be doing everyone a tremendous favour if he tested the device himself, right now, before something awful happened, like a fire, or skidding off the runway, or running out of complimentary pretzels?

The plane slowly started taxiing towards the runway.

Dammit, it was his *duty* to test this door! All their *lives* depended on it!

Before anybody could react, Fred unbuckled his seatbelt, lurched forward, grabbed the door handle, lifted and pushed.

The door performed exactly as engineered, propelling itself away from the plane while automatically deploying the bright yellow slide ramp. Fred sat back in his seat and marvelled at it all, as screams and shouts filled the cabin and the pilot jammed on the brakes, causing everyone to jerk forward hard against their belts.

Except Fred, who wasn't wearing his belt. He whacked his head hard into the seatback in front of him.

Highly-trained airport security boarded the plane and hustled a dazed, incoherent Fred (babbling "Well, at least you know it works!") away, not because they considered him a terrorist, but to protect him from hundreds of irate passengers whose travel schedules just got shot to hell.

Rachel was one of those irate passengers, and she was particularly pleased that, of the fusillade of flotsam flung at Fred, her full water bottle hit him square in the back.

For myself, I may only practice emergency procedures under strict supervision.

Fred & Rachel's Jamaica Mistaka

Decades ago, when Fred and Rachel got married and before Fred became infamous as the World's Worst Tourist, they wasted no time indulging in a time-honoured ritual of couplehood:

They had a raging argument. En route to, and during, their wedding reception. With parting shots at the subsequent dinner.

Fred's Best Man remarked to Rachel's Maid of Honour that this obviously meant they were made for each other. The MOH, who thought Rachel was nuts marrying a twit like Fred, smiled sweetly at the BM and dumped her cake in his lap.

Next morning, argument resolved, Mr. and Ms. Newlywed embarked upon their honeymoon: a flight to Jamaica and a sun-kissed resort therein.

For the first three days of their honeymoon, the Do Not Disturb sign hung constantly outside their suite. The housekeeper knew people were alive in there, because room service trays appeared outside their door from time to time.

On the fourth day, Fred and Rachel emerged into the blinding Jamaican sunlight, resplendent in their new bathing suits, and explored the resort. They cavorted in the warm Caribbean sea, gambolled along the sugar-white sand beach, and frolicked in the large swimming pool.

Actually, their pool frolicking often got quite heated, what with them being newlyweds and all. Especially at dusk, when most guests were either at dinner, or at the bar, and the pool was deserted, transforming into a serene magical place, lit only by its underwater lights.

During those twilight times, the warm water grew hotter with Fred and Rachel's torrid embraces. Above water, she kept her bikini top on to maintain some illusion of decorum. However, below the surface, her bikini bottom joined Fred's swim trunks at the bottom of the four-foot-deep pool.

After the third night of this amorous aquatic activity, which did not exist in any swimming manual, the lusty couple decided to get dressed and hit the hotel's bar for some pre-dinner tropical drinks.

It was their first time there. Yet as they descended the stairs to the below-ground bar, everyone greeted them warmly, as if they were old friends. The bar patrons were complete strangers to the young honeymooners.

As they made their way to the bartender, some men clapped Fred on the back in admiration, as if he had just won the Olympic Marathon or something. Other men leered at Rachel, while women giggled at both of them as they walked by.

Arriving at the long polished mahogany bar, the Rasta-man bartender greeted them so enthusiastically, that his wide grin almost split his ebony face. He said that because Fred and Rachel had been so good for his bar business, their drinks were on the house that night.

Fred stammered that he must have them confused with another couple, but the bartender boomed a deep laugh and said: "No, mon. No confusion at all."

Basking in this unfamiliar adulation, Fred ordered a pair of Mai Tais, then turned to his bride with a goofy grin on his face. His grin slowly faded as he saw Rachel, white-faced and still, staring open-mouthed at something behind him.

Fred swivelled on his bar stool to see what she was staring at. He too went white.

A huge underwater window took up most of the side wall. A huge underwater window that looked into the swimming pool, providing bar patrons with a crystal-clear view of whatever went on beneath the surface.

Fred and Rachel turned a red deeper than any sunburn.

They took full advantage of the bartender's hospitality that evening.

My own honeymoon was slightly more discreet.

Fred Invades Europe

Fred, the tourist most deserving of being on the No Fly list, and his stoic wife, Rachel, flew from Toronto to Germany, their first stop on a long-awaited European vacation.

They landed in Austria, having boarded the wrong flight thanks to Fred's bullheadedness. After much arm-waving consternation from Fred, and calm alternate arrangements from Rachel, they found themselves on a train bound for Munich, where their paid-for hotel room awaited.

En route, as Rachel gawked at the glorious Alps, Fred ordered a Schnapps. Or several. One for each Alpine peak, in fact.

Arriving at the vast Munich train station, a quite tipsy Fred insisted on handling their luggage himself, eschewing a porter, "to save money." After dragging their newly-purchased Scotsman TravelMiser suitcases half the length of the long train platform, he realized they had no wheels, something Rachel had been trying to tell him while he was busy shooing away porters.

Cursing, Fred picked up both suitcases by their handles and recommenced walking, griping about their immense weight, caused, he was certain, by Rachel's things (his, actually).

Finally arriving at the head of the platform, they saw two exit signs, at opposite sides of the cavernous station. Red-faced, perspiring, Fred asked, and not nicely either, where their hotel was. Rachel replied that it was just outside the station, and if he'd wait but a moment, she'd use her freshly-learned Berlitz German to inquire which exit to take.

Completely out of patience, Fred arbitrarily selected an exit and lumbered off with the suitcases, growling that the odds were 50/50 that he had picked the right one.

Emerging into the bright Bavarian sunlight, they looked around. No hotel.

Furious, Fred marched up to a cab and ordered the driver, in

English (having refused to learn any German), to load the suitcases in the trunk. He collapsed inside the cab with a great gusting gasp of relief.

Rachel followed, shaking her head, and gave the cabbie the hotel's address. He laughed and explained in German that it was just on the other side of the station. They had picked the wrong exit.

Fred refused to move. The cabbie explained again, this time in English, how close they were.

Fred glowered at him and stayed put. Rachel implored the cabbie to just drive there.

Muttering some German words that Rachel had not learned on her Berlitz disc, the cabbie very slowly drove them around the train station and, with immense disgust, deposited them at their hotel. When Fred wasn't looking, Rachel gave the man an outrageous tip.

After they had checked-in and Rachel left to go shopping, to soothe her embarrassment at travelling with a Neanderthal, an intoxicated Fred angrily called down to the front desk to complain that he couldn't re-open the microwave in their room. He was cooking popcorn he'd brought from Canada; he always travelled with snack food.

The front desk clerk, still learning English, haltingly explained that there were no microwaves in the rooms. Fred insisted there certainly was a microwave there, he had even closed the door and pushed the buttons, but now he couldn't get the damn door open again.

The clerk patiently repeated that the room had no microwave. Expressing his candid opinion of her command of English, Fred slammed the phone down and passed out on the bed.

He forgot about the incident when he awoke next day, being preoccupied with a throbbing head threatening to explode.

The following day, after Fred and Rachel had departed for their next international incident, the housekeeper was astonished to discover a bag of unpopped microwave popcorn locked inside the in-room safe.

Fred & Rachel Get Mortified

"What happens in Niagara Falls, stays in Niagara Falls"

Fred is one of those travellers that cause the locals to close their borders to tourists. Fred's long-suffering wife, Rachel, will definitely be canonized a saint after her death, despite being Jewish, for putting up with him.

On a trip to Vegas, Fred insisted on eating only at cheap buffets, "because it saved money for gambling." On a website listing the cheapest of the cheap, he found the lowest-priced one with this traveller's frank feedback on TripAdvisor: "Food: terrible. Open 24 hours, except for one hour a year when they close for cleaning." He ignored the comments.

After dining there, much of their "saved money" went to Fred's Vegas hospital bill, to cure a severe case of ptomaine poisoning.

Rachel visited him often, since the hospital had slot machines in the visitors' lounge. She won $1,000 and didn't tell Fred.

On another gambling excursion, Fred and Rachel visited Niagara Falls for two days. They never once saw the famous thundering cascade. They camped inside the Fallsview Casino.

Every hour, Fred tried a different sure-fire "system" on the slot machines. Every hour, Fred failed to hit the jackpot. Both his losses and temper mounted.

Meanwhile, Rachel, prudently ensconced in another part of the vast gaming mecca, invested $20 and reaped a return 100 times that. She stashed her winnings in the depths of a purse that could easily hold enough provisions for a five week Amazon trek, and went for a victory drink.

Next morning, after breakfast with an extra helping of Fred's grousing, they returned to their hotel room to pack. Rachel wasn't packing fast enough for Fred, who wanted one last try at changing his luck at the slots before driving home to Toronto. So he swatted her on the backside with his ball cap, to hurry her along.

Rachel gave an angry yelp of pain as the metal button in the centre of the cap impacted her buttocks. She glared at Fred, who apologized profusely. She emptied his packed suitcase onto the carpet.

Eventually re-packed, they left the room and went to the elevator. Fred pressed the down button and apologized again for inadvertently hurting her. As the elevator arrived and the doors swooshed open, revealing what appeared to be an empty conveyance, Rachel heatedly replied:

"Instead of apologizing, you should massage my sore ass!"

They entered the elevator and were shocked to discover two white-haired ladies pressed against the right-hand wall, considerately making room for whoever was boarding. They both stared open-mouthed at Fred and Rachel.

Omigod! What MUST they be thinking? thought Rachel, mortified.

She grabbed Fred, who was trying to exit, then smiled her sweetest smile and asked how the elderly women were enjoying their vacation. One acknowledged they were having a good time, while the other looked at Rachel's behind, then at Fred, who had turned deep crimson.

Forging ahead, Rachel asked where they were from. They warmed up, saying they were from Maryland and had just arrived in the Falls after two days sightseeing in Toronto. Rachel asked about what they'd seen there. An animated conversation ensued, as the elevator crawled downward with the glacial slowness of baggage handlers at Toronto's Pearson airport and Fred minutely examined the swirls in the wood panelling.

Finally reaching the lobby, the women bid goodbye as if they were old friends. Fred fled to the car with the luggage.

"Well, those ladies will have quite the story to tell their tour bus companions about their perception of Canadians' bedroom habits," smirked Fred when Rachel rejoined him.

She took off his cap and swatted him.

His "Ow!" pleased her immensely.

Fred's First Cruise

Some of Rachel's colleagues at work had taken Caribbean cruises and spoke glowingly of them, filling her head with visions of the pampered life at sea and visiting exotic island ports. So she arrived home from work one day, full of enthusiasm to book a Caribbean cruise. And ran straight into her husband, Fred.

Her ship was scuttled before it even cast off.

To say Fred was Mr. Negative would be akin to saying the U.S. national debt was negligible. He was adept at finding a cloud in even the brightest silver lining. He came up with every drawback to taking a cruise imaginable, and even a few that defied imagination. ("How do we *know* that Somali pirates haven't branched out into the Caribbean? Eh? Eh?")

Rachel moped for days and was on the verge of booking something with a girlfriend, leaving Fred marooned ashore with his negativity, when she won The Prize.

She had never won anything significant before in her life. Yet she won the travel prize in a hospital lottery of an all-expense-paid trip for two to cruise the Caribbean for a week aboard a luxury liner. The lottery folks called her at work with the joyous news.

In hushed tones of reverent awe, her co-workers still talk of her Happy Dance to this day.

Fred immediately dropped his objections upon learning of the all-expense-paid nature of the trip and announced that he'd accompany her. So it was that the World's Worst Tourist strode up the gangplank of the magnificent ship one month later, wife in tow.

And fell flat on his face as he stepped aboard.

He didn't see the slight ridge where the gangplank met the ship, and his size 13 shoe caught it, sending him flying. Just as the ship's photographer snapped that all-important "happy couple as they first come aboard" keepsake picture. (It's actually quite a photo: Rachel in the background smiling beatifically, while in the foreground Fred is falling forward so fast he's blurred, eyes wide in astonishment, mouth open in a goofy "O." She's got it framed on her office wall.)

This is an ominous beginning to our first cruise, she thought, as two crewmembers helped her husband to his feet, he muttering darkly about suing the cruise line for his bruised knees and elbows and ego.

Rachel was ecstatic when she saw their cabin: an elegant suite much larger than a standard cabin, with a capacious bathroom, big verandah, luxurious bathrobes, and a huge bouquet of flowers in a crystal vase on the coffee table.

Fred was ecstatic over the well-stocked mini-bar and promptly proceeded to take full advantage of it. (He continued to do so throughout the week, as their attentive Filipino room steward kept restocking the fridge as quickly as Fred emptied it. It actually became a contest between the two men.)

They had an entire day at sea before their first port of call, and they both flung themselves into the cruise life. Actually, Fred did most of the flinging. He flung himself at the all-you-can-eat breakfast buffet, the gorge-yourself-until-you-burst lunch buffet, and the groaning-table midnight dessert extravaganza. He flung himself into all three swimming pools, with wild whoops heralding expert cannonballs and belly flops, resulting in mighty splashes that soaked everyone sunbathing in lounge chairs poolside. He flung himself into the shipboard tennis tournament with such abandon that he was ejected from said tournament before the entire week's supply of balls disappeared overboard.

It was at dinner that Rachel put her petite size five foot down. She insisted they dine in the elegant formal restaurant.

"But, but you have to dress up for that!" protested Fred.

"Yes, and that's why I bought all those new outfits before we left. Outfits that I intend to wear," she replied firmly.

With Fred stuffed into the suit she'd forced him to pack, they went to partake of their first French cuisine gourmet dinner. In hindsight, Rachel should have seen it coming. After all, when Fred ate out at home, it was only at restaurants that met his discerning criteria: cheap food and lots of it.

As the uniformed waiter placed his main course in front of him, Fred took one look at the small portions and blurted: "Where's the rest of it?" Their table companions laughed, thinking he was joking. Rachel cringed inside, knowing he was not.

Fred escalated his complaint to the point where the maitre d' was summoned. With much derisive sniffing, a second dinner was fetched for the peasant at Table 85, who had already wolfed down the first serving.

The next night, as his entree arrived, Fred regarded the tiny, perfectly-prepared quail and snapped: "What the hell is this? I thought I was getting a big roast chicken!"

By the third night, there was a notice about Fred posted in the huge galley. His portion was noticeably larger than anyone else's in the entire dining room. However, as the white-gloved waiter materialized off his left side and began spooning sauce atop his meat, Fred snarled: "Stop playing with my food!"

For the remaining evenings, Rachel was happy to unleash Fred upon the graze 'n' grab dinner buffet in the casual restaurant, while she dined in the French restaurant with her grateful tablemates.

When the ship docked in San Juan, Rachel booked a tour of Puerto Rico, as neither of them had ever been to that island. Thanks to "unforseen developments" (eg: Fred), the tour bus was 20 minutes late returning to the ship. They were barely back aboard, when the impatient captain, fuming at the delay, ordered the crew to cast off.

Their next stop was the duty-free shopping mecca of St. Maarten, specifically the capital, Philipsburg. No shore excursion was booked; they intended to spend the whole day shopping. And shop they did. Well, Rachel did. Fred spent the day haggling.

He haggled over every purchase, even over a can of pop sold by a scrawny kid with a dripping cooler in the blazing sun. He haggled so much, that they lost all track of time. Finally, horrified, Rachel realized that their ship was due to sail in 10 minutes. And the dock was 15 minutes away.

"The captain was most insistent when he announced this morning that departure was going to be precisely at five o'clock," Rachel said, panic welling.

"Relax, babe," said Fred, determined to win this one last haggle for a pair of designer sunglasses. "He'll wait. Remember when our island tour was late yesterday? They waited. Besides, no one ever leaves on time."

"Japanese trains do," said Rachel. "And KLM, the Dutch airline. The Dutch are sticklers for promptness. And civil servants like yourself certainly leave the office right on time."

"Ah, don't worry. Our skipper's not Dutch," said Fred, ignoring her last remark. "I think he's Italian."

As they fast-walked toward their pier, burdened with parcels, they noticed a black cloud pouring from the smokestack. As they drew closer, they noticed a gap appearing between the ship and the dock.

"She's leaving!" wailed Rachel.

"STOP!" bellowed Fred.

As the ship slid further away from the dock under the influence of its powerful side thrusters, which churned the water into a white froth, Rachel turned on her husband with her own froth: "It appears our captain IS Dutch."

Fred dropped all the bags he was carrying and ran to the edge of the pier, waving his arms frantically. "STOP! COME BACK!" he screamed. He saw passengers gawking at him from the rails and redoubled his efforts.

"WAIT! Come ON! We're passengers! You can't leave us! STOP!" Sea gulls, startled into the air by his commotion, circled overhead, laughing.

"I'm a good TIPPER!" he lied desperately.

By this time, Fred was jumping up and down like a pro basketball player with fire ants in his britches. Onlookers were amazed at the heights he reached. "The NBA should sign that guy up," chuckled one observer, sipping his cocktail.

"STOOOOP!" Fred shrieked, leaping and gesticulating, as the colossal vessel moved inexorably away. Rachel, meanwhile, simply stood, shocked and immobile, still clutching her bags, staring at the receding ship as if willing it to reverse course back to the dock.

Tears welled in her eyes. Then she looked at her husband, cavorting wildly like a demented orangutan, and murder welled in her heart. *Our passports and airline tickets and all our stuff are on that boat. And here we are stuck in a foreign country with no documents.*

However all was not lost. A harbour official sauntered up to them and revealed that they were not the first passengers to ever be left behind. The cruise line had an arrangement for such instances: The ship would wait once it was outside the narrow harbour entrance, while a high-speed launch rushed them to her.

The hapless castaways and their many parcels were loaded aboard a sleek, low-slung launch, which roared off after the departed liner. When they caught up to her, the behemoth towered over them.

"How the hell are we supposed to get aboard?" said Fred, looking up at the skyscraper-sized sheer wall of steel.

He soon got his answer. One of the lower cargo hatches ponderously swung open and a rope netting was deployed down the side of the ship to their launch. With a big smile, their launch skipper told them to start climbing.

"I'll keep my boat next to your cruise ship, while my first mate holds the bottom of the rope net to steady it," the skipper said. The first mate, with a cheek-splitting grin as wide as his boss', bowed deeply, then took hold of the swaying net.

"What?!" yelped Fred. "You can't be serious!"

"Oh man up, for God's sake," gritted Rachel. She grabbed the net and started ascending. *Thank God I'm wearing shorts and not a skirt or dress,* she thought. Holding on for dear life, not once looking down, she climbed steadily and soon had helping hands grab her and assist her into the cargo hold. Cheers wafted up from the launch crew.

With much cajoling, Fred finally made his way up and inside as well. Their bags followed, all stuffed into a big net tied at the top. The launch pulled away, laughter from its crew mingled with the rumble of its powerful engine, and the big hatch clanged shut.

One hour later, a bill for the rescue was delivered to their room. When Fred saw it, he was apoplectic. "Three hundred dollars! For just a short boat ride! Outrageous! I'll see about this!"

He stormed off to the Guest Services desk in the cavernous central atrium and demanded to speak to the manager. The man told him, politely but very firmly, that it was his own damn fault for missing the ship and that was the cost of reuniting them with it. Fred tried to haggle, but got nowhere.

The manager explained that the ship had to leave its berth promptly at five, because they had a specific time to depart the crowded harbour. If they missed that time, they'd have to wait until all the other cruise ships departed before being granted a new time. That would mean hours delay.

"But how come you waited 20 minutes for our tour bus yesterday?" Fred demanded.

The manager said it was because the organized tour had been booked through their cruise line, so the ship had been obligated to wait for them. And San Juan's harbour didn't have a bottleneck at its entrance like Philipsburg, necessitating strict departure times.

Fred returned to their room, fuming. Rachel had dressed and left for dinner at that snooty French restaurant that served Lilliputian portions. He attacked the contents of their mini-bar with grim purpose.

The following day, they docked in Jamaica. Although they had visited that country before on their honeymoon, they rented a bright red Jeep to explore the island on their own (not having ventured from their resort on their first visit, being somewhat preoccupied). They found all sorts of back roads and secluded beaches to challenge the Jeep, which suited Fred fine, as he wanted to "get his money's worth" from the rental.

Bouncing along one rural road, they came around a bend and saw a rare stretch of straight road before them. It had rained heavily during the night, and a large, long puddle (a small lake, really; you could float a canoe in it) covered the road, just past the end of a tall, thick hedgerow that grew to the edge of the road.

"Puddle!" Fred yelled joyously and tromped the accelerator. The Jeep sprang forward. Screeching a banshee wail, he plowed through the puddle.

It was only after they cleared the hedgerow, just as they hit the puddle, that they saw the line of cars on the other side, parked facing inwards at right angles to the road. Three of the vehicles were mini-vans, with their rear lift gates open. A group of hikers - six men and four women - were standing at the open lift gates, gearing up for a nature hike along one of Jamaica's jungle trails.

Rachel, despite having her brains rattled by all the rough road and off-road jouncing, instantly recognized the dreadful implications. But it was too late.

An enormous sheet of water cascaded over the hiking party and into their vehicles in a tsunami deluge as the Jeep tore by. Fred continued speeding down the road trailing cries of shock and outrage in his wake.

Rachel stared at her husband, appalled. "You ... you *stew-pid IDIOT!*" she said, hitting him on the shoulder. "How *could* you *do* that?"

Fred gulped. "I ... I didn't even know they were there! I couldn't see past that hedge."

"Well, you just swing this Jeep around and get back there. You have to apologize and make amends."

"Aw c'mon, honey. Those guys are all big and muscular. They're in no mood right now to listen to any apology. They'd just pound me into mush! Besides, in this sun, they'll dry out quick."

He paused, struck by a sudden thought: "And I think I did those guys a helluva favour anyway. Didja see the tight t-shirts on those buff women? Now they're wet t-shirts!"

She hit him again - twice - and didn't speak to him for the rest of the day.

When Rachel returned to their cabin after another elegant dinner that night, she waited impatiently for her buffoon to reappear. She knew he usually went to the onboard casino after stuffing his face at the buffet. When he returned depended on how long his money held out.

Tonight, it wasn't long. Fred entered the cabin, took one look at his wife's stern face, and tried to beat a hasty retreat.

"No you don't. Get in here," she commanded.

He knew better than to argue with *that* tone. He shut the door and plopped down on the couch as she spoke:

"At dinner tonight, I overheard a group at the next table. They were complaining about some thoughtless jerk in a red Jeep who raced by them today when they were getting ready for a hike, right through a big puddle, soaking them to the skin. Sound familiar?"

Fred blanched. "Ah, so they were from this boat, eh? Ah, that's an incredible coincidence."

"Coincidence indeed. Here's another: not only were they from this boat, not only did I sit near them tonight, but one of them is a cop!"

"C-c-cop?"

"Yes, my insensitive moron. He said he gave a good description of the Jeep to the island police, along with a partial license plate number. As a professional courtesy, they promised to track it down by contacting the car rental agencies on Jamaica, and find out who was driving it. Then this cop plans to hunt down the S.O.B. responsible in his home country and demand satisfaction."

Fred sat with his mouth agape, speechless. Rachel glared at him and said: "Wages of sin, boyo. Get ready to pay 'em. Serves you right. I *told* you to go back right away. So you'll get no sympathy from me. In fact, I may turn you in myself, tomorrow night at dinner."

Fred looked out at their verandah and wondered if he should vault over the railing now and let the sea have him.

He stayed in his cabin all the next day, the last day of the cruise, ordering his meals through room service. He invented several kinda-plausible stories to explain what happened, and finally settled on this one: the Jeep's accelerator pedal got stuck. He convinced himself that Jeep was secretly owned by Toyota, to lend credibility to his stuck-accelerator excuse.

The last day of the cruise brought another shock for the World's Worst Tourist. When their bill arrived for incidentals bought during their voyage (a spa treatment for Rachel, wine and beer at dinners, souvenirs, a Lladro porcelain sculpture that had slipped from Fred's fingers as he examined it in the ship's gift shop), he discovered that his many in-room mini-bar charges were *not* part of their "all-expense-paid" trip. (He was never one to read the fine print.)

The mini-bar amount was eye-popping.

However, he had no opportunity to fret over it during their last night at sea. The patron saint of travellers arranged a temporary detente with the demon of lost luggage and the imp of surly service, and together they concocted a suitable penance for Fred for his puddle-jumping incident.

The ship ran into a major Caribbean storm, with winds and rain almost at hurricane force. Despite its mammoth size, and its underwater stabilizers, the ship bucked and wallowed through the enormous waves like an untamed bronc with a bellyful of loco weed.

By midnight, at least half the passengers were hopelessly seasick. Especially Fred.

As the tempest started affecting the ship, Fred raided their medicine cache. (The always-prudent Rachel, mindful of whom she had married, travelled with a drugstore full of medicines to cover any eventuality.) First he installed a seasick-prevention bracelet on each wrist. Then he downed some Gravol. As mal-de-mer built within him, he downed more pills, exceeding the maximum recommended dose.

Didn't work.

He then applied the contents of three boxes of Transderm skin patches - six patches in all (the stipulated dose was one).

Still didn't work.

He spent the entire night in an intimate relationship with their toilet, hurling until there was nothing left to hurl, then retching some more.

Rachel, blessed with a cast-iron constitution, would have

slept on a lounge chair on their verandah to escape hearing Fred's wracking heaves, if it weren't for the pounding rain and shrieking wind.

By six o'clock the next morning, as the ship nuzzled against its dock within the calm, protected harbour, Fred was white as a sheet and weak as a kitten. Accordingly, he was a model passenger on their flight home, falling asleep even before the jet's wheels bid farewell to the tarmac.

Fred's first cruise was not his last, as you'll read later in this book.

"It is not fit that every man should travel;
it makes a wise man better,
and a fool worse."

– William Hazlitt

Fred's Wild, Wild North

Fred, the World's Worst Tourist, and his wife Rachel drove north from Toronto all the way up to Cochrane, Ontario, and only got lost three times (Fred being one of those omniscient drivers who knows more than any stupid map or GPS device).

Fred had seen an ad with a jaw-dropping photo of two kids swimming with a full-grown polar bear at Cochrane's Polar Bear Habitat, and he just had to do that too. Since the Toronto Zoo flatly refused to let him swim with their polar bears, that meant a trek north.

Arriving (finally) at the Habitat, the road-weary couple paid the admission and Fred donned his swim trunks. Rachel would watch from the gallery; she was kinda leery about swimming with the largest carnivore on the planet.

Entering the pool, Fred discovered that a clear plexiglas wall separated tasty tourists from behemoth bruins. Creative marketing: You could swim *with* the bears, but not *among* them.

Fred got so upset that Security ejected him.

Horrified at the prospect of listening to Fred complain all the way back to Toronto, Rachel scoured guide books for something to amuse him en route. In Timmins, she found the Canadian Wildlife Park.

Part of the Cedar Meadows Resort, the 175-acre Wildlife Park featured native Canadian animals, including herds of moose, elk and bison. You could feed an adult moose (less traumatic than a polar bear feeding on you).

Upon arrival, they clambered aboard the resort's large tractor-drawn passenger wagon, the tractor coughed into life and, with considerable swaying and jouncing, they toured the Park.

They really did feed fresh-cut branches to a full-grown moose. Rachel was allowed out of the wagon to stand next to the animal, which towered over her while gobbling the branch she timidly held. (The guide had intuitively classified Fred as "risky" and insisted he stay aboard the cart to feed the moose.)

Later, they encountered bison. The snorting, temperamental beasts crowded around the wagon, sharp horns gleaming in the afternoon sunlight, as the guide fed them from a bucket of grain. Ordered to stay safely ensconced in the high wagon, the tourists took pictures.

Fred, miffed at not being allowed out to feed the moose, angry at not being able to swim among polar bears, decided he was going to get his close encounter with iconic Canadian wildlife no matter what, dammit. Besides, this was a park, so these critters were tame, right?

A hulking male bison stood next to the wagon, its snout buried in the grain bucket. With years of watching the Calgary Stampede on TV under his belt, Fred vaulted over the side and landed on the creature's back, straddling it.

"Yee-HAW!" whooped the armchair cowboy.

Time froze. For one second.

Then everything happened at once. The guide exclaimed some very choice words. Rachel screamed. The bison realized some foreign matter had landed on its back.

And Fred realized these animals were not tame.

The big bison bellowed and bucked. Fred found himself airborne, sailing over the massive head and crashing into a tree. The guide heroically placed himself between bison and buffoon, as it lowered its horns for a charge. He distracted the agitated animal while unconscious Fred was heaved onto the wagon by two fast-moving fellow tourists.

The park owner agreed not to press charges if Rachel agreed to keep her husband far away from Timmins. Fred, nursing a concussion, had no say in the matter.

Driving them home, Rachel wished Fred *had* been allowed to swim among the bears. In fact, she would have paid double.

Fred's Last Resort

A tale of Fred & Rachel's earlier years

Paula, the owner/operator of a quaint cottage resort in the Kawarthas, had been an innkeeper for two decades. She had developed an almost-infallible instinct about her customers, able to size them up between the time they stepped out of their vehicle and when they had walked up the path to check-in at her office.

She got a terrible feeling about her latest guests before they even got out of their car. It happened as soon as they drove up. Plastered across the entire rear window of their battered, rusty compact car, in bold pink letters, was:

"Save the Ta-Tas." A big pink breast cancer ribbon was between "Ta" and "Tas," as if that made the phrase all right.

Two couples in their early twenties unfolded out of the car. The twosome from the back seat were fairly ordinary-looking. So was the female front passenger. It was the driver (and, she found out at check-in, the car's owner) that set Paula's alarm bells clanging.

A tall gangly scarecrow, his face seemed permanently etched with a vaguely confused expression, which reminded Paula of a quote from one of her favorite authors, Mark Twain: "He looked like an envelope without any address on it." (During weekdays in winter, when there were few, if any, guests at her resort, she devoured books of all types and sizes.)

Despite his facial expression, he sported an air of self-importance, an attitude of "I know everything that needs knowing." He wore a black t-shirt that complemented the decal on his car's back window. In big white letters, it read: "I (heart) BOOBIES." Although a small pink breast cancer ribbon was printed next to the heart, Paula suspected that the guy wore it for prurient reasons. She sighed and shook her head.

In stark contrast, his lady had an affable demeanor. She was also completely different physically (besides being female, that is): she was so short, she barely came up to his chest.

At the front desk, the mis-matched couple introduced themselves as Fred and Rachel. Their backseat travelling companions were Bob and Michelle. They had all just graduated from college and had rented a two-bedroom cottage for a week to chill in the Great Outdoors, before starting the serious task of looking for full-time jobs.

Oh great, thought Paula as she handed them the key to Cabin 5 and cheerily waved them off. *College grads out to party at MY resort. Joy.*

She watched as equal parts luggage and cases of beer were unloaded from the cramped little car and hauled into the cabin. *Wonderful.*

Their first night, the couples were up until the wee hours, talking loudly, singing ribald songs, and playing some party game that generated shrieks of laughter from the women and bellows of guffaws from the men. Paula went down and pounded on their door three times during that long night, pleading for them to tone it down so their neighbours could sleep. Was about as effective as the federal government's Long Gun Registry in curbing street crime.

Next day, in early afternoon (they only awoke around noon), Fred decided they should avail themselves of the resort's complimentary watercraft. He shambled past the line of waiting canoes, pedal boats and kayaks, and jumped onto the spotlessly-clean pontoon boat moored at the dock. It took some doing, but Fred eventually got the chain off the boat, while Bob got the engine going (no mean feat, since the former was padlocked and the latter had no key in the ignition). Joined by the micro-bikini-clad Rachel and Michelle, carrying a full cooler of beer between them, they cast off and motored up the lake with Fred at the helm.

About an hour later, Paula approached the dock, accompanied by a gaggle of guests that had signed up for Paula's Perfect Perambulation sightseeing tour of the lake. Paula stopped abruptly. Her boat, her beloved and meticulously-maintained pontoon boat, was *gone*.

She scanned the lake anxiously, but her boat was nowhere in

sight. The padlock showed obvious signs of being forced open. She called the local OPP Marine Unit on her cell phone, to report the theft. Turned out the aqua-cops were way ahead of her. Far up the lake, they had stopped a pontoon boat emblazoned with the name of her resort. They discovered that beer was being consumed aboard (against the law on boats that are not moored and don't have a galley and a head). Luckily, Cap'n Fred hadn't been drinking, otherwise the boat would have been seized and his drivers licence suspended.

After gracing Fred with a hefty fine and confiscating the booze, an officer was driving the boat back to the resort, trailed by his partner in the OPP marine cruiser, when Paula's call came in. When the little flotilla arrived, and Paula realized that it was her own guests who had absconded with her vessel, she withdrew the stolen property complaint.

After the OPP had departed, she furiously berated the couples for taking her boat without permission. Fred, already seething about his fine, shouted that the resort's brochure stated that watercraft were complimentary.

"You didn't read it carefully!" retorted Paula. "It clearly states NON-POWERED watercraft. That means the canoes, kayaks and pedal boats! The CLUES were that my boat was padlocked with no ignition key! There's a charge to rent my pontoon boat and it includes ME as skipper with NO alcohol aboard."

Fred stormed off, muttering about "fine print" and "false advertising." Rachel made profuse apologies, and shepherded Bob and Michelle away from the irate innkeeper, who looked like she was ready to commit bodily harm. That look intensified when the innkeeper discovered the seats in her boat were smeared with sun tan oil.

The following day, in early afternoon, Paula was making tea and a sandwich in her kitchen, clad only in her underwear as she had just doffed her grubby gardening clothes inside the back door upon entering her house. She was admiring her backyard flower and vegetable gardens through the kitchen window, when a tall loose-limbed man ambled up to her prized pear tree in the centre of her yard. He plucked a pear from a branch and took a huge bite.

She went to her screen door and shouted: "Hey! Those are my pears! And you have no business being in my backyard!"

The man - Fred - finished chewing, swallowed, and said, affronted: "I assumed, as guests, that we have the run of the resort. There's no sign here saying 'Private' or 'Keep Out'."

"That's because the only way to get into my fenced-in backyard is through my house!"

"Nope. You can also get here through your garage. Your garage door's open, y'know. And by the way, while I appreciate the view, shouldn't you be wearing a robe?"

Paula remembered she was standing there in her underwear. With a muted curse, she stepped away from the screen door, while bellowing:

"Scram!"

Late that night, as Paula made the rounds of her resort prior to turning in, she was startled by a tent-ripping belch coming from Cabin 5. She looked and was horrified to see someone - obviously a male - standing on the cabin verandah urinating over the side!

"Hey! Stop that!" she thundered. "My lawn is not your toilet! Use the bathroom in your cabin!"

The man zipped up and turned to face Paula, blinking in the light of her flashlight. *Ah. I shoulda known*, she thought.

Fred.

He said that their bathroom was in use and he just HAD to go. Paula said that hers was a clean family resort and NOT for use as an outdoor toilet.

"Aw, c'mon lady," said the obnoxious dimwit. "You allow dogs here. When they do their business, what's the difference?"

"Guests with dogs must walk them along a path through the woods that I created just for that purpose. Dogs aren't allowed to relieve themselves anywhere else. So if you simply MUST pee in the Great Outdoors, feel free to use the dog path!" She stomped off into the night, clenching her teeth so hard, she got a headache. Behind her departing back, Fred gave her the finger.

Fred's *magnum opus* came the following evening.

At dusk, looking out at her resort from the raised deck attached to her house/office/gift shop/games room/video lending library, Paula noticed flames shooting into the sky down at the beach and thought: *A bonfire? But there's no fire pit there. In fact, that's where the -*

"Holy crap!" she exploded, and charged out of the house. She ran to the beach and skidded to a stop in the sand, jaw dropped, eyes bulging, appalled.

The lamebrains from Cabin 5 were sitting around a massive roaring bonfire, with flames leaping three and four feet high. A massive roaring bonfire built in one of her horseshoe pits!

"What the HELL do you think you're DOING?" she screamed. "My brother from Nova Scotia helped me build those horseshoe pits last spring! They're perfect regulation pits! They're NOT for bonfires!"

Fred looked at her and said: "Huh. I tho't t'was your fire pit. Shore licked like one t'me." His words were slurred; the bottles in the sand around the foursome testified why.

"I *told* you it was a horseshoe pit," hissed Rachel, glaring at Fred. "Moron."

"My fire pit is over THERE," Paula gritted, pointing. "Did you not notice the three-sided border around this pit, made of beautiful cedar timbers, or the tall metal stake in the centre? Did that not give you a HINT that this is for horseshoes?"

"Uh, no." He hiccuped. "Ma'am."

A red rage flooded Paula. With supreme self-control, she ordered them to extinguish the fire, which they did by heaping sand on it. (Fred wanted to douse the flames with Bob "in the manly way," but both Rachel and Michelle firmly put a stop to that.)

Paula returned to her house, having remembered that she had a gun from her duck-hunting days with her father long ago. She intended to put it to good use, that very night.

But she couldn't find any buckshot shells.

Early next morning, she roused the hung-over blockheads in

Cabin 5 and turfed them off her property.

"But, but you can't evict us!" Fred protested, his head throbbing. "We're paid up for the whole week! We haven't drunk all our beer yet!"

"I can and I am," Paula replied. "My poor resort couldn't survive whatever stupidities you come up with during the rest of this week. Last night's ruined horseshoe pit was the last straw! I've had quite enough of you! I'm keeping your rent for the three days you have left as compensation for all the damage you've done here. So pack up and leave! You. Are. TURFED!"

Rachel prevailed upon the others to depart speedily and without hassle, though Fred loudly groused the entire time they were packing. As their car roared off down her country lane, spewing rocks and dust in its wake, Paula muttered an apt observation made by Oscar Wilde 100 years ago: "Some cause happiness wherever they go; others, whenever they go."

From then on, her family, friends and regular guests referred to her as The Turfinator.

She made a point of notifying the provincial Quaint Cottage Resort Association, giving them Fred's name, address and description, asking that it be circulated to all members with a warning not to rent to him. *Ever.*

Little did she know that she had just experienced the debut of the World's Worst Tourist. If she had, she'd have looked harder for those buckshot shells.

It would have been a blessing for the global tourism industry.

Why innkeepers get grey ...

Fred Goes Bird-Watching

There comes a time in every Canadian's life each winter, when we get fed up with snow, cold, more snow and more cold. Even the antics of our self-absorbed politicians fail to provide relief.

That's why God created the Caribbean islands.

So it was that Rachel, desperate for hot sun and swaying palms, stuffed suitcases and husband Fred *(Travellis horribilus)* aboard a plane bound for Cuba.

That idyllic isle does have a few rules, however. One such: Because they are a devout Catholic nation, no topless women are allowed on Cuban beaches. Hearing this upon arrival at their resort, an immense sadness overcame Fred and he immediately hit the bar to research exactly how many Mojitos it took to become cheerful again.

Rachel stoically went to their room, unpacked, slipped into her brand-new bathing suit, and hit the beach. Where she discovered a wonderfully-relaxing lounge chair underneath a palm tree, and a wonderfully-attentive waiter named Humberto, who kept her well-supplied with Margaritas, served with the most brilliant smiles.

Because of his intensive research at the bar that first day, Fred didn't leave his hotel room for the next two days. For Rachel, it was the most relaxing two days she'd enjoyed in ages.

Day Three dawned and Fred felt well enough to explore the resort. He wandered hither and yon, noting the strategic locations of every bar and bikini. Then he chanced upon a section of beach that was an outstanding habitat for bird-watching.

That's what he told Rachel, as he zoomed past her palm-shaded lounger en route back to their room for his camcorder. Rachel looked up from her novel quizzically, as the only birds that Fred had ever expressed interest in were found at restaurants smothered in gravy.

For the rest of that week, Fred alternated between dips in the sea, bar-hopping and bird-watching. Each evening over dinner, when Rachel inquired how his bird photography was going, Fred said he was getting some amazing footage and changed the subject.

On their last day, as he deposited another perfect drink, Humberto asked why her husband never joined her under the palm tree. Rachel replied he was often bird-watching and pointed down the beach.

Humberto exclaimed: "Ah, *si!* He goes to the European Beach!" Then he walked away smirking.

Rachel immediately left to find this "European Beach."

Rounding a rocky outcropping, she came upon the area in question and noticed several things:

1. The entire beach was full of well-oiled females, ranging in age from teen to don't-ask, and every single one had misplaced their bikini bras.

2. It was the safest beach in Cuba, as the resort's entire security force, devout Catholics to a man, were patrolling the perimeter by lurking behind palm trees, the better to protect the baking beauties from perverts.

3. Some bushes overlooking the beach were moving out of sync with the sea breeze, with occasional flashes of sunlight reflecting off glass. Highly-polished glass. Like camera lenses.

Upon further investigation, Rachel discovered that one of the lenses belonged to a camcorder held by Fred, who went incredibly red when confronted by his wife.

"Bird-watching INDEED," snapped Rachel, as she ordered husband and camera out of the bushes and back to the hotel. She confiscated the film.

Halfway home on the return flight, Fred realized the bushes had contained a Caribbean variety of extremely itchy Poison Ivy.

Rachel had such a grin when they landed, that the Customs officer had difficulty matching her face to her dour (as mandated by law) passport photo.

Fred Goes Fishing

Herb, Fred's friend at work (actually the only one there who could tolerate him), booked a week-long wilderness fishing trip in Labrador. When his next-door neighbour, the intended fishing buddy who knew all about the sport and had promised to teach him, suddenly couldn't go because he'd tried to get rid of a wasps' nest without wearing protective gear, Herb asked Fred to accompany him. (It was poor Herb's last resort; none of his other friends could go, the trip was paid-for and non-refundable, and even promising to do the housecleaning for a year failed to persuade his wife to spend a week in the deep woods far from a decent bathroom.)

Fred's wife, Rachel, tried to warn Herb about her husband's well-deserved reputation as the World's Worst Tourist (several countries even had him on their Banned Undesirable Morons list). Herb, desperate, ignored her. Rachel, used to being ignored by her lawfully-wedded idiot, suddenly realized she'd be Fred-free for an entire week, and walked away with a Cheshire Cat grin that threatened to split her cheeks.

So it was that, mere days later, a float plane loaded with far too much gear skimmed down a Northern Quebec lake whose waters finally, reluctantly, released its pontoons. Engine howling, the plane hauled itself into the early-morning sky, bound for Labrador. On board, Fred and Herb grinned bravely at each other, while their French-Canadian pilot wondered how long these two Toronto *anglais* would last in the bush.

The plane deposited them on the shore of a remote, pristine lake teeming, their pilot assured them, with *beaucoup poisson*. He unstrapped their canoe from a pontoon and helped them set up camp, including pitching their enormous tent (large enough for a family of eight, plus pets). Then he flew off, promising to return in three days to check on them.

The first two days were largely uneventful. Despite their woeful inexperience, they actually managed to catch some fish (Fred hooked himself four times while casting, and only flipped their canoe twice). They then discovered neither of them knew how to properly skin and filet their finny feast. Fred, having seen a documentary on the subject, insisted on doing it. The result looked like something already half-chewed and only remotely resembled anything fish-shaped. Of course, it didn't matter how unappetizing the fileted fish looked; after Fred got through cooking it over the blazing campfire, it was inedible.

Thankfully, their wives had insisted they bring a good supply of canned food.

They also made the acquaintance of their wilderness neighbours: About a million of them, traveling in dense clouds that voraciously descended upon any bare skin. Mosquitoes. Each as big as your thumb. Our intrepid campers ran out of bug spray by the end of the first day. Herb increased the number of cigarettes he smoked, and Fred took up smoking and coughing, since the noxious blue-grey clouds kept most of the bloodthirsty pests away.

Luckily, they also discovered each had thoughtfully packed enough Scotch to drown a moose, and further discovered that liberally lubricating their insides made the bites on their outsides tolerable. Ditto their cooking. And their jokes.

Late in the evening of the second day, as their roaring fire finally expired because all the dead and almost-dead wood within 100 yards had been consumed, the two besotted outdoorsmen decided to call it a night. They stumbled into their tent, singing ribald shanties and giggling like schoolgirls.

They wormed into their sleeping bags, doused the Coleman, and spent another hour telling insipid stories and lame jokes, while finishing off the day's second bottle of hooch. Then Fred realized he had to visit the outdoor plumbing.

He fumbled out of his bag, jammed his feet into his Kodiaks (left foot into right boot, right foot into left), unzipped the tent fly, and staggered outside. An almost-full moon lit the forest. Fred careened away from the tent towards a likely-looking tree.

His shovel of a foot caught on a tree root, sending him lurching forward, arms flailing. Fred abruptly found himself somersaulting down the steep hill towards the lake.

His rapid descent came to a sudden end when he landed on his back in their beached canoe with a mighty crash of seismic proportions and a scream loud enough to wake the dead. Which it did, as Herb jolted out of a drunken stupor with an alert, intelligent "Whazzah?"

Which meant Herb was awake to marvel at the sight of huge sharp claws slashing through the back wall of their tent.

A male black bear had been snuffling around behind their tent, trying to decide if the noisy, noisome numbskulls inside were worth eating. Fred's sudden crash 'n' scream had scared the bruin, who reared up on his hind legs and slashed the tent wall into ribbons.

The pale moonlight gave Herb an excellent view of the big bear through the gaping hole. Herb let out a high-pitched girlish shriek that rivaled any B-movie actress victim. The bear, scared again, roared its defiance, turned, and loped away into the woods as fast as it could galumph.

Herb realized he would need to wash out his sleeping bag come morning. So he swapped it with Fred's.

He left the tent and eventually located Fred, sprawled almost-senseless in the canoe. He helped his fellow angler/drinker/smoker/bungler back up the hill into the tent. Wordless, they gawped at the lacerated wall. Then they realized they no longer had a barrier between them and the mosquitoes, who wasted no time descending upon the buffet now available to them.

Both men scrambled back into their sleeping bags, burrowing deep inside. They eventually discovered they needed fresh air to breathe, and so poked as little of their faces out as possible.

They passed a terrible night. Dawn found them huddled around the campfire; said fire smoking as much as they were.

An hour after dawn, twin silver pontoons kissed the mirror-still waters of the lake and the plane taxied up to the shore. The pilot swore in both official languages, plus Cree, at the sight of Fred and Herb's ruined faces. Their eyelids were almost swollen shut, their lips looked like a botox treatment gone horribly wrong, and every inch of skin bulged with multiple bites.

Then all three discovered that the bear had been at their food cache before it had trashed their tent. Last night after dinner, they had hung their food up a tree in a big nylon sack. The bear, far cleverer than humans gave it credit for, had merely slashed the rope holding up the sack, then after it had answered the call of gravity, devoured or destroyed everything in it.

With one exception: An entire carton of smokes had vanished. For whatever unfathomable reason, the bruin had taken it.

"Huh," said Fred through puffy lips. "Guess we were robbed by Smokey the Bear."

Both Herb and the pilot pelted him with mauled provisions.

Conservation Officers of the Newfoundland and Labrador Department of Fish, Wildlife and Icebergs have since received reports of a nicotine-crazed black bear terrorizing campsites, seeking cigarettes.

Fred & Rachel Survive a Plane Crash

The big 747-400 lifted off the runway at Los Angeles, bound for Hong Kong. Originating in Toronto, the 416 passengers aboard the packed flight were mostly Chinese, with a few token whites mixed in.

Fred and Rachel were two of the token whites. Rachel was travelling to Hong Kong on business, while her husband was going to visit Hong Kong Disneyland, the only Disney theme park he had yet to pester with his presence. (In fact, he was now on the Do Not Admit list of five of the other nine Disney parks.)

The mammoth jet climbed to 43,000 feet over the Pacific and set a course for Hong Kong. Thirty minutes later, it ran into extremely-strong headwinds. The pilot changed altitude several times, but could not escape them.

The plane started burning twice as much fuel than expected, just to maintain its cruising speed against the vicious headwinds.

Aboard the aircraft, Fred was living up to his renown as the World's Worst Tourist. After harassing every fellow passenger within earshot and most of the smiling, unfailingly-polite Chinese flight attendants, Fred received a personal visit from the co-pilot, who sternly informed him that he would be restrained and drugged if he didn't sit quietly for the rest of the flight.

Fred slouched in his seat, glowering. Rachel, sitting next to him, continued to pretend she was travelling solo.

As the long overnight flight droned on, most of the passengers fell asleep, Fred included. Rachel, who could never sleep aboard a plane, kept reading her novel, a murder mystery about a wife who offs her husband while cleverly disguising it as an accident. She was intrigued to see where the wife went wrong; what tripped her up so the handsome, astute police inspector could catch her. She considered the novel to be an educational reference.

So it was that, long hours later, Rachel was awake to hear -

nothing. The familiar throaty roar of the four jet engines abruptly ceased. The loudest sounds were snoring passengers (Fred among the loudest), and the eerie whoosh of wind rushing past the fuselage.

Rachel sat up straight and craned her head to look around the darkened cabin. Several rows away, a man's head likewise popped up to gaze about. The man left his seat and came over to Rachel. Tall and lean, he wore a blue USAF uniform and identified himself as a Lieutenant.

"You too must fly frequently to have noticed the change in sound," he said.

"Yeah, I fly a lot on business," Rachel replied. "It sounds like the engines have stopped."

"That's almost correct, ma'am. They're all idling. We're now gliding. The change in sound woke me up right away. Something's wrong. There's no way the pilot would idle all four engines mid-flight."

At that moment, the full cabin lights came on and the flight attendants started going down the aisles, awakening everyone. Then the PA system crackled into life and the pilot made an announcement. In Mandarin. Then he repeated it in Cantonese. Finally in English:

"Excuse me, ladies and gentlemen. Due to the very strong headwinds we have been battling almost our entire flight, we have just about run out of fuel. However, there is no need to be concerned. We are rerouting from Hong Kong to Tokyo, Japan, to refuel. Then we will continue on to our final destination. We apologize for the inconvenience."

A low buzz of conversation followed the announcement, but no one was overly alarmed. Unscheduled refueling stop. No big deal. Back to sleep.

Rachel felt the gliding plane angle downwards. Dawn was breaking as they descended through the clouds. Through her window, she saw the blue Pacific far below. No land was in sight.

As Rachel kept watching, the blue Pacific got closer. Much closer. So close, that she could now see whitecaps. Still no sign of any land whatsoever.

The co-pilot came over the PA, and his announcement was again delivered in three languages. This time, however, the screaming and crying and shouting started after the first one in Mandarin. By the time he switched to English, the plane was in an uproar:

"Apologies again, ladies and gentlemen. It now appears we will not be able to reach Tokyo as we had hoped. We must now make an emergency landing on Okinawa Island. Yes, please consider this to be an emergency landing. Please ensure your seatbelt is securely fastened and assume the crash position. We will be landing very soon."

Rachel gasped and looked out her window again. She still couldn't see any land, but the whitecaps now looked close enough to splash the plane.

She heard the wheel bay doors whine open and the landing gear lower. She tightened her belt and bent forward, saying a quick prayer.

That's when Fred woke up.

Quickly appraised of the situation by his bent-over wife, Fred reacted calmly and coolly, the epitome of a seasoned traveller.

He started screaming like a schoolgirl at a pop star concert, and pounded the seat back in front of him.

Rachel looked out again and *did* see water splash the wing of the impaired aircraft. Then the wheels hit something solid with a colossal *BANG*. The pilot immediately threw his engines into full reverse. After so long a silence, the angry roar of the four powerful Pratt & Whitney engines was deafening. He also applied every ounce of braking power the plane had.

The effects in the cabin of the harsh touchdown and emergency deceleration were immediate and devastating. Anything not secured went flying. All the overhead bins snapped open and their contents, most of which were heavy, cascaded downwards upon the helpless passengers. Shrieks of pain filled the cabin.

After three seconds, the howling engines all flamed out with loud pops. The fuel tanks were now bone dry.

The pilot grimly kept braking for all the plane was worth, because he knew something the passengers didn't: The Okinawa airfield was of WW II vintage and was much too short to accommodate a huge 747-400.

The 231-foot-long aircraft quickly ran out of runway and slid into the marshland beyond. Everyone discovered that if there's one sure way to stop a speeding 747 quickly - guaranteed - it's to plunge it into marshland.

As the mucky bottom gripped its massive tires, the plane came to a sudden and complete stop. All the fallen baggage from the overhead bins swept forward, smashing into people and bulkheads like missiles. Along with one adult passenger who, unbelievably, had not secured their seatbelt.

Fred.

He had been sitting three-quarters of the way down the cabin and now found his screaming self on an impromptu airborne tour, hurtling towards the forward bulkhead. He clipped several seats en route before crashing into the bulkhead. He collapsed in a tangled heap, amazingly still very much alive, as evidenced by his bellows of pain.

The shaken flight attendants did their highly-trained duty. They opened all exit doors and deployed the bright yellow inflatable escape slides. They started sending passengers down the slides one by one.

When it was her turn, Rachel kicked off her shoes and, not giving a damn how her skirt rode up, quickly slid down into the waiting marsh. She stood up and found herself thigh-deep in smelly, brackish water. She hastened away from the slide, her stockinged feet squishing into the ooze of the bottom.

Fred was the last passenger to slide off, due to his injuries. He came down sideways, shouting imprecations against the pilots for gross incompetence, and hit the marsh water backwards. Coughing and spitting, he clutched his left arm as he stood unsteadily, and needed help to move away from the mired aircraft.

Deposited a safe distance away, Fred's first thought was not of Rachel, or of the other passengers, or his injuries. His first thought was of his lawyer, to file suit against the airline. He fished out his cell phone. His wail of anguish joined the hubbub of crying and groaning all around him.

His cell was kaput, having been thoroughly soaked by the swamp water.

Emergency personnel soon arrived, including medical teams. Upon examining Fred, they found he had a badly-bruised arm and multiple bruises along his body. However, they discovered his left leg had a compound fracture.

Rachel had a sore shoulder, courtesy of a flying bag. But she considered herself lucky; many other passengers, particularly those with aisle seats, had sustained far worse injuries from the heavy items formerly residing in the overhead bins.

A series of smaller planes flew everyone from Okinawa to Tokyo that afternoon, where they received full medical attention. They kept Fred heavily sedated, to silence his constant complaining.

Two days later, Fred and Rachel were in Hong Kong, where Rachel kept her rescheduled business appointments. Meanwhile, Fred still insisted on going to Hong Kong Disneyland, despite his plastered leg. Once there, he discovered a little-known benefit of visiting a Disney park in a wheelchair:

He was immediately whisked to the head of the long line-up for any attraction he cared to ride on - no waiting!

In addition, since his Caucasian features made him stand out in a sea of Asians and out of pity for his disabled state (which Fred milked for all it was worth), he was selected to be Grand Marshal in the noontime parade down Main Street. The crowd cheered wildly as Fred rode by on the lead float, smiling and waving, since they figured he was some famous Hollywood movie star. In fact, a rumour swept through the mob that he was Johnny Depp.

Fred had started the rumour.

"Airline travel is hours of boredom
interrupted by moments of stark terror."
– Al Boliska

Fred Discovers Tequila

Fred, the World's Worst Tourist, and his long-suffering wife, Rachel, took advantage of a great package deal and jetted off to Cancun, Mexico.

They stayed at a sprawling all-inclusive resort with wonderful amenities: all-you-can-eat buffets, all-you-can-drink bars, all-you-can-see white Northern skin barely covered by micro-bikinis. Plus: friendly staff, sports, shows, spa, and on-call medical help.

Fred, habitually sedentary at home, felt compelled to demonstrate his he-man prowess at all of the resort's sports activities: water polo, sailing, snorkelling, kayaking, jet skiing, para-sailing, volleyball, horseback riding, archery, and tennis. (The fact that he had never done any of these sports before deterred him not a whit.)

Fred got to know the on-call doctor real well. As did the poor guy in charge of the archery range. And the group Fred crashed into while para-sailing.

The horse had to be treated for post-traumatic stress disorder.

They never did find the jet ski.

Rachel, meanwhile, swam in the sea, relaxed in a lounge chair under a swaying palm, and pretended she was there by herself.

Every night, the main bar had a table full of differently-flavoured tequila shots. The first night was lime-flavoured tequila. The second night, apricot. Then cherry, then citrus, then cinnamon.

Fred, being Fred, had to try each and every one. Many times. Each night, he declared that flavour to be the "best ever." Each night, he had to be carried back to his villa, while Rachel sipped her margarita and enjoyed the stage show.

On the sixth night, they served jalapeno tequila. With a real pepper floating inside the bottle.

Fred started downing shots. Pingo, the bartender, knowing

el loco quite well by then, kept the bottle handy to refill Fred's glass.

Eventually, the bottle nearly empty, the jalapeno pepper fell out as Pingo poured. Fred grabbed the glass, but Pingo intervened.

"No, no *senor*! You do not want to eat that pepper! It is *muy* hot! Trust me, *amigo*. Let me pour you a shot from a fresh bottle."

Fred snorted: "Ah, don't worry, buddy. Back home, I eat half a Costco tub of feta-stuffed jalapenos every week in one sitting. This little pepper won't bother me one little bit."

With a piratical grin, Fred drained the shot, pepper and all. He chewed lustily and swallowed.

His grin faded. His face reddened. His mouth dropped open. His eyes bulged.

"OmiGOD!" Fred yelled. "I'm on fire inside! Gimmie water! *Agua! Agua!*"

Fred's face was now beet red. Tears coursed from his eyes. People nearby swore they could see steam coming from his ears.

Pingo hastily started filling a high-ball glass from a frosty pitcher of water. Fred grabbed the pitcher away from him and started gulping water directly from it, oblivious to the ice cubes cascading down his chest. He drank as if he'd been in a desert for a month.

People started throwing coins at Fred's feet, thinking he was the night's entertainment.

"More *agua!*" he gasped, when the pitcher was drained. "I'm dyin' here!"

Rachel had seen the whole thing and was dying herself. With laughter. Her face was as red as Fred's and tears also streamed down her cheeks.

After another pitcher, Fred's five-alarm fire became a smouldering burn. Commandeering a third pitcher, Fred stuck a straw in it and joined Rachel at their table. With dignity, he started sipping. Rachel took one look at him and convulsed in hilarity again.

The following night, Pingo greeted Fred with a huge smile:

"*Hola, senor!* You were *muy* funny last night! Would you like another pepper shot? People have come to my bar tonight just to see your next performance."

Flushing pepper red, glowering, Fred ordered an unsweetened ice tea and sat at a table in shadow at the back of the bar.

I, too, have learned never to eat what's floating in a tequila bottle.

The Haunting of Fred

For all her bright enthusiasm and savvy business acumen, Rachel had several phobias: spiders, small enclosed spaces, aggressive panhandlers, and her in-laws. But her biggest phobia, the one that had afflicted her since early childhood, was:

Ghosts.

She had a pathological fear of spooks, which had been caused by her father. He saw no reason why his beloved daughter, all of five years old, shouldn't enjoy the gruesome, terrifying ghost movies that he loved so much. Young Rachel had nightmares for days after each viewing.

As an adult, her phantom phobia was so bad that she wouldn't even go on the popular family-fun *Haunted Mansion* attraction at Walt Disney World. For her, the worst time of year was Hallowe'en. She let Fred answer their door that night, while she stayed in bed under the safety of her covers.

As a reward for a hugely successful marketing campaign which she had created and implemented, her company sent her to the annual convention for professional marketers. There, she heard a powerful, invigorating speaker discuss the secrets of a fulfilling life, which started by facing and overcoming one's fears. Naturally, the only way to effectively implement his success strategies, was to buy his set of eight instructional DVDs, three CDs, 400-page workbook, laminated pocket/purse card, and engraved brass key ring. She was so taken by him, that she did.

After faithfully going through his entire self-help program, she decided to tackle her greatest terror head-on. So late in October, she booked two tickets for a Ghost Walk. Along with the World's Worst Tourist, she travelled from Toronto to Peterborough to partake of it.

The Ghosts 'n' Gore Hallowe'en Walking Tour started at 9:00 p.m. and lasted 90 minutes. Participants were guided through

Peterborough's historic downtown. The tour's website had promised that haunted places would be visited, replete with spooky tales of the past: murders, suicides, executions, and accidental deaths, all narrated by a knowledgeable tour guide from the local historical society.

Normally, Rachel wouldn't have been caught - ahem - dead within a mile of such a tour. However, fortified by that charismatic speaker's slick (and expensive) self-help program, she was determined to confront and conquer her worst phobia. Besides, Fred would be there to help her through it.

She never suspected that Fred had his own agenda for that evening.

It was a dark and stormy night *(what an original line!)* the evening of the Ghost Walk. A strong wind howled through the almost-deserted downtown, chasing occasional droplets of rain. Dark clouds scudded across the sky, often obscuring a baleful werewolf moon. Bundled up in her fall coat, with a tartan beret crammed on her head, Rachel shivered and it had nothing to do with the chill autumn air.

Their tour guide was a stout woman of indeterminate age with wind-whipped greyish hair that insisted on escaping her hooded black cloak, framing her lined face with questing tendrils like Medusa's snakes. She carried a flickering black lantern containing a thick candle, and her cracked booming voice contested with the keening wind as she addressed the group of 20 brave Ghosthunters.

As the tour worked its way through the alleys and lanes of downtown, Fred acted on his hidden agenda. His low opinion of the existence of ghosts, goblins, ghouls and other creatures that go bump in the night, was exceeded only by his even-lower opinion of self-help gurus. He was determined to have his fun with Rachel who, he believed, had now wasted their money twice: once on the self-help kit and now on this stupid Ghost Walk.

As the tour stopped at each allegedly-haunted site, and as their guide mournfully related the gruesome death that supposedly caused the haunting, Fred did his best to add to the atmosphere.

Standing in the darkness behind Rachel, who listened with rapt attention to the guide, he moaned in low tones, softly at first so she thought it might be the wind, then gradually louder until, with a start, she whipped her head around, only to find her husband also listening to the story, his face innocent, expressionless.

This continued through several stops, and Fred was gratified to see her become ever more nervous. His goal was to send her into terrified hysterics, whereupon he would smugly announce that he had caused all the supernatural effects, thus proving two points: Ghosts did not exist and self-help gurus were charlatans.

(It never occurred to him that it would also prove a third point: He was a mean, insensitive jerk.)

As the tour wore on and tales of macabre demise multiplied like cadavers during the Black Death, Rachel thought Peterborough surely must be the most haunted city in Ontario. She could feel her tight self-control slipping. Fred continued to assist the process. When the tour group entered buildings, he sometimes blew at her hair while they stood in darkened rooms above taverns and shops, or in hundred-year-old stairwells lit by a single feeble light. He made worn floorboards creak and closed warped doors slowly so the hinges squealed. Once, he knocked a rusty can off a cobwebbed windowsill in an abandoned apartment when no one was looking. Rachel jumped with a tiny squeak.

His masterpiece came when they descended into a dank cellar below a sparsely-populated bar and huddled amidst kegs of beer and dusty broken furniture. The cavern was pitch black, save for the fitful light cast by the guide's lantern. Rachel stood at the edge of the group, and Fred stood behind her; both completely shrouded in darkness. Their guide related the horrible tale of a youth sent down here 70 years ago to fetch a keg, who had been crushed when a stack of heavy kegs fell on him.

"They say his ghost haunts this place still, and at a certain hour, the poor lad touches any person unlucky enough to be down here, in mute supplication for assistance.

"And that hour is right NOW!" cackled their guide.

Fred bent forward and grabbed Rachel around her ankle with

one hand. She shrieked.

He forgot that his wife had taken a martial arts self-defense course.

Rachel spun around and delivered a perfectly-executed roundhouse kick that caught Fred right on the chin. He was unconscious before he hit the ground.

Screaming, she bolted for the stairwell, dimly-lit by the light from the open cellar door up on the main floor. The rest of the group hastily followed, their guide bringing up the rear, shouting for calm. They pounded through the bar past gawking patrons and out the front door into the street beyond. Fred was left crumpled on the earthen cellar floor in the dark, forgotten.

The Ghost Walkers entered a brightly-lit coffee shop four doors down from the bar, and fortified themselves with cappuccinos, lattes and teas. Rachel, shaking, downed a hot herbal tea so fast she barely tasted it or noticed how it scalded her mouth. She promptly ordered another, oblivious to her husband's absence.

Fred slowly regained consciousness. Nursing his jaw, he fumbled his way towards the stairs. Despite his fall jacket, he was shivering due to the time he had lain on the cellar floor. Just before he stumbled up the stairs, he grabbed a big tablecloth from a stack on a shelf and draped it over him for warmth.

At the head of the stairs, he noticed a rear door. He exited through it, finding himself in a narrow alley behind the row of shops, bars and restaurants lining the street out front. Still dazed, he started walking toward the alley entrance, pulling some of the white tablecloth over his head for added warmth.

Ahead of him, a door opened into the alley and the Ghosthunters emerged, re-fortified by caffeine. Their guide had ushered her charges out of the coffee shop's rear door, as their next stop was further up the alley. Rachel was the last to emerge.

She had no desire to continue with the tour. But she was in an unfamiliar city late at night, and had no clue how to get back to where their car was parked. Plus, she had finally noticed she was Fred-less and hoped he'd rejoin the tour at some point.

She shut the door behind her and started walking to catch up with the group. Suddenly, she heard an eerie sound behind her. It was a low, guttural moan, exactly like that of some malevolent apparition. (Or a husband who'd had his jaw kicked and couldn't talk too well at the moment.)

She whipped around. Her eyes bulged. A tall spectral shape, all in white, was shambling towards her, arms outstretched, moaning like the damned. She screamed, rooted to the spot. The gaunt phantom came closer, ever closer, groaning ever louder, pale bony hands reaching for her, a black hole where its face should be.

Rachel screamed again, completely terrified. Her knees felt like water; her legs refused to work.

She heard "Oh, for God's sake!" as a bulky black shape brushed past her and descended upon the ghastly spectre. She saw their tour guide wallop said spook hard with her lantern, right on the head. The creature of the night collapsed without a sound.

With an oath, their guide bent and whisked off the white shroud enveloping the alleged spirit.

Rachel gasped. "FRED!"

Rage flooded her. "You, you *bastard!*" she yelled. "You thought it'd be fun to play a trick on me, knowing how hard I worked trying to overcome my phobia! So you dressed up as a ghost and waited in this alley to scare me, eh? You utter *bastard!*"

When Fred regained consciousness, the Ghost Tour had vanished, including his wife. In their place were flashing lights, ogling onlookers, two policemen, and an EMS unit tending to his injuries. Once treated, he was driven off to jail, charged with being a public nuisance.

He couldn't understand why Rachel never came to bail him out. His lawyer had to drive all the way from Toronto to do it.

It was over a week before Rachel spoke to him again. And when she did, her words weren't very nice.

They took separate vacations for the next year.

Normally, the Ghosts 'n' Gore Tour is much more sedate. Except for that time when the Headless Window Washer appeared.

Fred Goes on Safari

In Animal Kingdom, at over 500 acres the largest of the four theme parks at Walt Disney World in Florida, a major attraction is Kilimanjaro Safaris. There, real African animals (not Disney's famed audio-animatronics) seemingly roam free over a 100-acre scenic savanna, while visiting humans ooh and aah from the safety of big open-air safari trucks jouncing over a rutted road.

One day, in the rearmost bench of one such truck, leaving at 8:00 a.m. on the first safari of the day, sat Rachel and the World's Worst Tourist. As the truck rumbled away from the loading dock, bound for the wilds of Africa, the driver cautioned everyone to remain seated at all times, and to secure hats, purses, bags and small children since the ride was going to be quite bouncy.

As Rachel stuffed her hat into the pouch fastened to the seatback in front of her for that purpose, she pointedly looked up at Fred's Tilley hat. He noticed.

"Aw, don't worry about my trusty Tilley," he said, tugging it down to his sail-like ears. "I've got it stuck tight."

"Uh-huh. Shouldn't you at least use the chin strap that Mr. Tilley thoughtfully provided?" she asked.

"Naw. Makes me look dorky. Besides, there's hardly any wind."

Rachel bit back a comment that it wasn't the chin strap that made him look dorky, and settled back to enjoy the ride.

Their vehicle entered the vast grasslands and its passengers marvelled at the plethora of animals: elephants, hippos, rhinos, lions, giraffes, zebras, impalas, antelopes, gazelles, mandrills, wildebeests, kudus, warthogs, cheetahs and more, including dozens of different birds.

The truck rounded a bend and started accelerating down a hill. They went over a particularly large bump and many people, especially those in the rear seat, briefly became airborne. Fred's head snapped back as he bounced out of his seat, just as a strong gust of wind blew across the savanna.

In a split-second, Fred's beloved Tilley hat was whisked off his head. With a cry of surprise, he spun around in his seat (as soon as he regained it) to see it waft away behind them on the breeze, then settle gently in the middle of the road.

Fred was thunderstruck. That hat had faithfully accompanied him on countless (mis)adventures all over the world, and now it was gone, just like that! Doomed to end its life either ground into the dirt by the succession of safari trucks that would travel this road today, or, even more ignominious, chewed and eaten by some jungle beast.

No! I can't just leave it there! he thought wildly.

He saw himself vaulting over the thigh-high door to the ground below (which was awfully far below since the truck bed was quite high off the road), oblivious to the screams of his fellow passengers and the unDisneyfied curse of the driver, who saw in her rear-view mirror that an unexpected buffet for the carnivores had just been deposited.

He landed hard, but his long legs absorbed most of the impact. He ran towards his precious hat, ignoring the Voice of Reason in his head that said: *Yo. Fool. Is your damn hat worth getting eaten?*

He scooped up the hat, brushed off a bit of dirt on its brim, plopped it on his head, then turned and saw -

Nothing.

His safari vehicle had disappeared around another bend. *Huh. They really meant it when they said the truck would stop for nothing.*

Looking around, he saw that the big male lion formerly lying atop his Pride Rock had risen and taken a keen interest in the pale-skinned newcomer to his domain. Three lionesses, the principal hunters in a pride, materialized next to him, also intently staring at Fred. He gulped, realizing how small - and edible - he was compared to the vast plain and its myriad denizens.

He saw that the lionesses, all sleek and tawny and undeniably skilled at what they do best, were now slinking down the hill toward him.

He was distracted by a low rumbling growl behind him. Whirling, he saw a huge black rhino pawing the dusty earth, waving its massive head, its sharp horns menacing in the early morning light. Fred remembered their driver saying the black rhino, and this was an adult weighing over 2,000 pounds yet capable of running at 35 miles per hour, was highly endangered.

Not as endangered as ME right now! Oh WHEN will the next truck arrive?

The lionesses were quite close now, and the rhino looked like it would charge at any moment. Fred wondered which would get to him first. Death by fang and claw, or horn and hoof? A mewling whimper escaped him.

"Fred! Fred, don't worry. Stop whimpering."

It was Rachel. In the safari truck. Holding tight to his arm. Preventing him from leaping over the side.

"A park ranger will drive over and pick up your hat. Our driver already radioed it in. They don't want foreign objects in the park, 'cause it could be harmful to their animals. We're supposed to stop by Guest Services at the entrance to Animal Kingdom later today to reclaim your hat."

Fred stared at her as reality flooded in. He had never left the safety of the truck! He was not about to be eaten or gored!

"Hey, Fred, you okay?" she asked, staring at him.

"Uh, yeah. Yeah, sure, of course. Guest Services, eh? Huh. Bet they just say that to keep us calm for the rest of this ride. Bet I never see my Tilley again. Elephant's probably already eaten it."

"Two words: Chin. Strap."

When the ride was over (their driver glared at Fred with an I-told-you-to-secure-your-hat look as they exited), they stopped in the gift shop and purchased a khaki-coloured Kilimanjaro Safaris ball cap, to protect Fred's balding head.

They enjoyed the rest of their day at Animal Kingdom, despite Fred's frequent grousing that he'd never set eyes on his favorite hat again. Finally, as the park was closing, foot-sore and exhausted (and soaked, courtesy of the Kali River Rapids attraction), they presented themselves at Guest Services. By this time, Negative Fred had conjured a veritable black rain cloud over his head.

After describing his lost hat in a mournful Eeyore tone to the smiling Disney "Cast Member" behind the counter, Fred was astonished when the person entered a back room and moments later emerged holding his hat.

"I don't believe it!" he said, stunned. "And look, there isn't even a tire tread across it! I was sure there would be, from the trucks that followed us."

Beaming like a child on Christmas morning, Fred whipped off the souvenir safari cap and reinstalled his Tilley on his head.

"Now look," he said. "I feel you should refund me the price of this ball cap. After all, I only wore it for the one day, today. It's not too sweaty. I should be able to return it."

The Guest Services rep gaped at Fred, open-mouthed.

"I've got the bill right here," said Fred reasonably, fishing out his wallet.

Still smiling, albeit tightly, the Disney employee stated that would not be possible. As Fred's querulous voice rose, Rachel rolled her eyes heavenward and slipped out the door, to peacefully admire a flock of exotic birds in a nearby exhibit and pretend, as she often did, that she was travelling solo.

Fred is not the only one to ignore the warning to secure one's hat on that safari ...

Fred Gets Taken for a Ride

After years of hinting and outright haranguing, Rachel finally persuaded Fred to accompany her to England for two weeks, to visit her relatives. It's not like she wanted the World's Worst Tourist along; her relatives insisted. They wanted to see for themselves the incredible twit they had heard so much about.

What enabled her to convince Fred to cross the pond was her assurance that there was literally a pub on every street corner in Britain. Which turned out to be a mistake. He insisted on imbibing in every public house they encountered during their travels, and many times her relatives happily joined them there. Which was rather fortunate: It meant that Rachel had plenty of assistance to help her cart Fred home and pour him into bed, as his tolerance for alcohol was akin to a Liberal's tolerance for a Conservative.

As Rachel's relatives were scattered all over England, the smartest, most efficient method of visiting them was to travel by train. They purchased BritRail passes that gave them unlimited travel for their two week sojourn.

Or so they thought.

While she was busily hugging and kissing her first batch of relatives goodbye, Fred went off to the wicket to buy the tickets. They discovered they did not have unlimited-travel BritRail passes one week later, when the conductor on the train they were on archly informed them that their tickets had expired.

Fred, having visited several pubs en route to the train, plus the pub car on board the train, was somewhat belligerent upon hearing this news. He insisted their tickets were still valid, as he distinctly recalled buying passes good for two weeks.

"Oh aye? Well, these are nowt fortnight tickets, sunshine," said the conductor. "An' I'll thank you not to be breathin' so close to me face. You've had a few. Now you'll have to pay for your passage, me lad, or I'll be puttin' you both off at our next stop."

Rachel dug out her wallet from her cavernous purse and asked to buy two tickets. Fred loudly instructed her not to, saying there was no way he was paying twice for the same ride. Seeing where this was going, she bought one ticket for herself then sat back in her seat, leaving her cantankerous tipsy husband to continue his own debate with the conductor.

Fred, now doubly incensed, proceeded to get into a raging argument with the BritRail official. Each man only understood half of what the other was saying, since each spoke a foreign language (British, specifically from Yorkshire, and Canadian, specifically from "Taranna").

As the train pulled into a station heralded by much bell-clanging, the squabble had degenerated into a red-faced shouting match on both sides. However, one side forgot that the other side had the power.

Fred found himself unceremoniously kicked off the train, and none too gently either. His bag was quickly located and flung out after him, thumping hard onto the train platform.

Rachel, mortified, slunk down in her window seat and flushed crimson. She should have kept some embarrassment in reserve for what came next.

Picking himself up, Furious Fred ran back to the train, yelling and waving his fists. The conductor stood in the open doorway, arms crossed, immobile, scowling, muttering some choice Yorkie observations about foreigners.

Cursing a blue streak, Fred unbuckled his belt and, turning away from the train, yanked down his trousers and Stanfields. He presented the conductor with a full Canuck moon. Rachel, hearing shocked gasps and laughter from her fellow passengers, looked out.

"OmiGAWD!" she said.

Unimpressed, the conductor flipped Fred the reverse-V British bird, turned on his heel and entered the train car.

To ensure he made his point in the most forceful manner possible, Fred backed up and shoved his pale backside against the window of the door, just as said door swooshed closed.

The train started pulling out.

That's when Fred discovered the train door had closed on part of his trousers.

He found himself being dragged down the platform half-naked, and crab-walked sideways as fast as he could to keep up. His crabby gait was hampered by the trousers around his ankles, which noosed tighter as the train accelerated. He was unable to free his big feet from the clothes. He started yelling and pounding on the door.

He reached the end of the platform and was jerked out onto the tracks. The train dragged him about 200 metres down the tracks before finally stopping.

Somehow, miraculously, he escaped serious injury. He was covered in cuts, some of them deep, and bruises. The police arrived soon after the ambulance, and announced to the semi-conscious bleeding tourist that he faced a large fine and several charges.

"It's a miracle your damn fool husband wasn't badly hurt," the constable told Rachel, who didn't know if she should be laughing or screaming at her idiotic mate. "This sort of thing can end up killing you. What the bloody hell possessed your man to do such a stupid stunt? Is he barking mad?"

Rachel smiled and said: "Oh yes."

Then a thought struck her. She looked at the cop and inquired if her husband would be jailed, perhaps for several days, until formal charges were laid and bail could be arranged. It would allow her to finish her British holiday by herself, in a sane and serene manner.

The constable regarded her, then it was his turn to smile. "Right you are, mum."

No conductors were harmed in the crafting of this story, although two elderly ladies who got a good look at Fred's lunar landscape fainted dead away.

Fred the Baker

Rachel reached that stage in her life when she wanted more than her successful marketing career and stoically enduring her inane husband, Fred. So she took up painting.

To provide inspirational fuel for her new hobby, she rented a charming seaside cottage in PEI for two weeks in late Spring. She arrived from Toronto with great hopes, enough artistic supplies to make Michelangelo drool, some clothes, and the World's Worst Tourist.

(She had tried in vain to convince Fred to stay home, but he felt he too deserved a break from his vague government job, which involved harassing innocent taxpayers for unnecessary forms, in triplicate. The truth, unbeknownst to Fred, was that his boss had called Rachel and begged her to take Fred with her, so the office could enjoy two solid weeks of increased productivity. A collection among his co-workers quickly raised money for his plane ticket.)

Fred figured that while Rachel painted the scenery and communed with nature, he'd chill out in a lounge chair on the beautiful red sand beach, surrounded by the soothing sounds of surf and sea gulls, cold drink at hand, and catch up on his reading. (He had caused quite a scene at the airline check-in counter when they surcharged him for his overweight suitcase crammed with books.)

He was bored out of his mind in three days.

Their rented cottage came fully-furnished. After sticking his nose into every cupboard, closet and cranny in the place, desperate for a diversion, Fred finally descended on the kitchen (usually a place he avoided, unless it was to raid the fridge).

Thus it was that, tucked away in the back of a large cupboard, Fred discovered the breadmaking machine. Scattering pots and pans to the floor with a cacophony of clanging loud enough to rouse a comatose senator, he hauled out the bulky rectangular machine. Seeing it festooned with many buttons and an LED screen, he was hooked.

Fred had never made bread before in his life, nor had he ever expressed any inclination to do so. To him, food preparation either meant waiting for Rachel to cook something, or driving ahead to the pick-up window. Yet the prospect of spending another 10 days at the isolated cottage simply doing nothing filled Fred with a hitherto-unknown baker's zeal that rivalled his obsession not to miss a single NHL hockey game on TV.

Placing the big machine on the counter, he lifted the lid and found a bread recipe book and the instruction booklet for operating the device. Flipping through the former, he selected a tasty-sounding (to him) recipe: Green Peppercorn Mustard Rye bread.

Because everything is better with mustard, he thought. Scribbling down the ingredients, he jumped into their rented car and drove off to the local grocery store.

They had found the store soon after arrival, and bought supplies to stock their larder. You had to turn right as you exited the lane leading to their oceanfront retreat. Fred turned left. He drove halfway around the picturesque Isle of Anne before stumbling onto another foodstore. (The thought of stopping and asking for directions never once entered his largely-empty head.)

Eventually returning to their cottage (he missed the entrance to their lane twice), he thumped his bags of bread fixings onto the kitchen counter. Knowing Rachel had packed a picnic lunch and hiked down the beach for the day with her easel and other artsy stuff, Fred had the whole afternoon to create a culinary masterpiece. (Note how "masterpiece" has precisely the same number of letters as "catastrophe.")

Knowing absolutely nothing about making bread, Fred ground his teeth in frustration as he followed the recipe instructions, since following instructions went against every fibre of his male being. Creating the dough was a laborious process. You had to place the many ingredients, which included water and three types of flour, into the machine's bread bowl in precisely the order dictated by the recipe, and woe be you if the yeast, the final ingredient, touched the water before the device was ready to mix it.

Convinced the recipe needed improving, he added raisins, cheese and chives to the mix.

When it was finally done, about an hour later (twice as long as it should have taken and with considerable spilled flour - all three types - coating counter, floor and Fred), he closed the cover of the breadmaker with a sigh of triumph.

Then he realized he now had a whole new set of instructions to follow, to work the device. After a cursory flip through the pages, he tossed aside the instruction booklet with a snort.

"How hard can it be?" he muttered, eyeing the instrumentation deck. "It's just a machine and I've operated many machines before." (The pile of ruined mechanical devices laid to rest in their garage graveyard back home was mute testimony to that. At work, his expertise with the department's combination copier/ scanner/collator/fax/microwave/coffeemaker had resulted in six such machines in two years. Fred's boss thanked Buddha she'd had the foresight to buy an extended warranty.)

He pushed some likely-looking buttons. The "on" light glowed and mysterious whirring noises sounded deep inside.

"It's alive! It's alive!" shouted Fred, exultant.

Some minutes later, the breadmaker beeped, then started chugging and vibrating, as the two interior paddles kneaded the dough. The device now sounded like someone relentlessly pull-starting a lawnmower that refused to start, and it shook like a dog shaking water off its fur. However Fred saw, through the observation window, that the mixing paddles were doing their job, turning the diverse ingredients into a big gooey ball of dough. He concluded that everything was operating normally.

Immensely proud of himself, Fred stepped out onto the porch to enjoy the view and see if he could spy Rachel returning home, ready to be suitably impressed with her man's latest accomplishment. She was nowhere in sight.

The recipe directions stated that it would take the machine

about three hours to bake his three-pound loaf, so he knew he himself had three hours to loaf. (Never once did he consider spending some of that time cleaning up his mess.)

From the kitchen came a tremendous crash.

Fred charged in and saw the breadmaker lying on its side on the floor. The device had bounced around so hard while kneading the dough, that it had walked itself clear across the counter and made a death leap to the floor, yanking its power cord out of the wall socket as it fell.

The suicidal machine had burst open upon impact, ejecting the bread pan. The fat ball of dough was rolling away to freedom on the kitchen floor.

Dismayed, Fred grabbed the dough and brushed off the more obvious bits of dirt and dust bunnies. *What Rachel doesn't know, won't hurt her,* he reassured himself.

He plopped the dough back into the pan. He quickly set the machine upright, then replaced the pan inside the breadmaker and lowered the lid. It wouldn't close properly. The machine's self-destructive plunge had dented the metal lid liner; there was now a big gap on one side of it.

Fred knew exactly what to do to rectify this situation; a solution hard-wired into every male.

From his earlier exploration of the cottage, he had noticed a toolbox in one of the closets. He ran for the closet and galloped back to the scene of the crime with a firmly-gripped hammer in hand. He beat the metal lid back into shape. More or less.

A tiny gap still remained and the now-battered lid looked like it had been attacked by crazed mutants in a post-apocalyptic movie, but it still looked better than before. Besides, time was running out. He closed the lid, heaved the machine onto the counter, and plugged it back in.

"Damnation!" our erstwhile baker exploded. "I was too slow!"

The LED screen indicated the device had reset its cycles, leaving our hero with half-kneaded bread. In a quandary, Fred set the machine for high speed cooking and pressed the start button.

With noises that sounded suspiciously like grumbling, the breadmaker clicked, beeped, and resumed its ministrations. Not taking any chances, Fred perched on a kitchen stool and watched the infernal device like a gambler fixated on the spinning dials of a slot machine.

It grunted, wobbled, vibrated, and took several hopeful steps towards the cliff edge of the counter, but Fred pulled it back from the brink each time. "You don't die on my watch," he growled.

It suddenly reminded him of the possessed hopping toaster in *Ghostbusters II*, except instead of pink poltergeist slime, his machine was obviously filled with demonic dough. He wondered if the cottage rested atop an ancient haunted Indian burial ground.

The breadmaker beeped again, waited quietly for awhile, then heated up to full intensity. The wholesome smell of baking bread soon filled the cottage. Though the paddles had finally stopped kneading, the boxy device still quivered sporadically.

Just as he was starting to relax, the lid abruptly blew off, smashing back on its hinges against the side of the breadmaker with a loud *BANG*. From a sitting position and with a surprised expletive that must be edited out for sensitive readers, Fred jumped two feet straight up from his stool, an athletic accomplishment worthy of an Olympic medal.

Knowing the bread wasn't cooked yet, he slammed the lid closed and encouraged it to stay-the-hell-closed with several good whacks from the hammer. The baking cycle continued.

About 20 minutes later, he noticed the wonderful baking smell was becoming tinged with another smell. A slight burning smell. A slight burning smell that grew steadily stronger.

When the first wisps of smoke wafted from the little gap remaining in the cover, Fred realized he had another problem. His precious bread was burning!

He started jabbing buttons, trying to turn the machine off or reset the high speed cooking cycle. Nothing worked. Smoke was now pouring from the breadmaker. Finally, desperate, he unplugged the beast. The smoke continued.

He couldn't get the cover to open. After another mad dash to the closet and a frantic rummage in the toolbox, Fred attacked the cover with the business end of a large flat screwdriver, assisted by encouraging taps from the hammer. As the encouraging taps grew stronger, the recalcitrant cover finally popped open, releasing a cloud of smoke in his face.

Coughing, he donned oven mitts and extracted the bread pan. His inaugural loaf didn't look anything like the photo in the recipe book. Instead of a light-brown, rectangular, high loaf with a rounded dome top, it was blackened, deformed and squarish with a squat depressed top except for one end, which had managed to achieve some height. It looked like a miniature overly-toasted ski hill.

Prying out the alien loaf and turning it over, he saw that the paddles had been baked right into the bread! (They were supposed to have been removed before the baking cycle began, as clearly outlined in the instruction booklet that Fred had ignored - that's why the machine had paused between the kneading and baking cycles.) Muttering dark imprecations, he excavated the plastic paddles, leaving two large, deep craters in the bottom of the loaf.

Fred pulled off some of the hot bread from the bottom, where it wasn't blackened, and gingerly tasted it, fearing the worst. To his surprise, it actually tasted pretty good. He pulled off some more and slathered it with butter. That made it taste even better.

When Rachel The Artist returned around dinnertime, to a quaint seaside cottage smelling of baked and burnt bread, she found the half-eaten misshapen loaf on the kitchen table and the detritus of the breadmaking experiment strewn about the kitchen. Stunned that her kitchen-phobic husband had actually cooked something, she sampled a piece of the now-cold loaf. It tasted pasty and undercooked.

Ugh. This would sit very heavy in my stomach if I ate any more, she reflected.

She found Fred locked in the bathroom, paying the ultimate price for scarfing down half a loaf of undercooked bread in one sitting.

When they checked-out of the cottage 10 days later, the

breadmaker had been cleaned and reassembled and returned to its dark berth deep in the kitchen cupboard. With a bludgeoned cover that now needed copious amounts of duct tape to seal it closed.

Moral: Support your local baker! It's safer.

*"If everything seems to be going well,
you have obviously
overlooked something."*

– Murphy's 8th Law

Fred & Rachel Get an Eyeful

At some point during a Canadian winter, one half of a couple looks intently at the other half and declares they have had enough of snow and cold and if they do not get somewhere south and warm forthwith, they will do something crazy, like listening to opera on radio or voting for the Green Party. The other half of the couple, if they value their personal safety, would be wise to promptly book a southern sojourn.

So it was that when Rachel gave Fred *that* look and announced that a cruise would be very welcome *damn soon*, the World's Worst Tourist wasted no time booking an escape to places where the water wasn't stiff.

Fred being Fred, he hit the Internet to find the cheapest cruise.

"Online is where you find the best last-minute sell-off deals at ridiculous prices," he declared as he worked the keyboard.

"Don't care, long as it's warm. Only white on the ground that I want to see are sand beaches," Rachel gritted as she fiddled with the radio dial, her left eye twitching.

Fred found a Caribbean cruise at a price so low it smacked of government subsidy. The only drawback: The ship would sail the next afternoon. Rachel let out a whoop and disappeared into the bedroom. She was packed and waiting impatiently by the front door within 30 minutes.

During the taxi ride to the airport, they both left voicemail messages for their respective bosses with creative reasons why they would suddenly be AWOL for the next week. ("Yeah, uh, my mother's best friend's step-dad's cousin just died. Mauled by a llama. Just horrible.")

Despite several incidents during the flight and transferring from the airport to the ship (Fred being Fred), they eventually found themselves ensconced in a windowless interior cabin that redefined "snug." After unpacking their suitcases into cupboards with less space than their suitcases, they trooped outside to a railing to supervise the ship's departure.

It was 20 minutes after cast-off, when they were surrounded by the azure Caribbean and enjoying a *bon voyage* drink in one of the vessel's many bars, that they heard the Cruise Director identify himself over the PA system and then make this curious announcement:

"Okay ladies and gentlemen, you can now take off your clothes."

Rachel looked at Fred, raising an eyebrow. Fred shrugged: "Weird shipboard humour." He signaled for another drink.

Later, they strolled the Lido deck where the ship's swimming pools were located to enjoy the fresh sea air and warm sunshine (and to satisfy Fred's secret agenda of ogling babes in skimpy bikinis). They were astonished to see acres of glistening well-oiled flesh of both genders - without a stitch of swimwear.

"They're ... they're all completely *naked*," whispered Rachel as they walked past.

"Yeah, and they're all so *old*," muttered a disappointed Fred.

"Totally gross," agreed Rachel. They hastily returned to their shoebox cabin.

They knew they were in a very unusual situation after they changed for dinner and presented themselves to the tuxedo-wearing maitre d' at the elegant dining room. They couldn't believe their eyes as they were escorted to their table.

Every diner was sitting on a towel, stark naked. Every diner looked at Fred and Rachel strangely, as if they had showed up at a funeral dressed for a New Year's Eve party.

"What the hell is going on around here?" Fred demanded of their waiter, thankfully also in uniform. "I thought you had a dress code for dinner. On my last cruise, I was asked to change from shorts to long pants before I was allowed entry to the fancy restaurant. Now look at this!"

The waiter smiled and informed them that the entire ship had been booked for this cruise by an international society of nudists.

He left them sitting open-mouthed without asking if they wanted wine with their meal.

Rachel recovered first, glaring at her husband. "You pervert! You booked us on a nudist cruise just to satisfy your puerile interests!"

"N-No! I ... I honestly didn't know!" Fred stammered. "I was just looking for the cheapest price. The website stated this was a cruise for a naturist federation, but I thought naturist meant people who enjoyed nature and wildlife and such. Y'know, tree-huggers."

"No, moron. That's what nudists call themselves."

Half-way through her appetizer, Rachel leaned forward and hissed: "Well, I'm certainly not going to parade around in the buff." As if reading her husband's mind, she added firmly: "And neither are you, boyo."

After dinner, they tracked down the Cruise Director, who confirmed what their waiter had said and added, to their horror, that the average age of the nudists was 80. That made the fortysomething Fred and Rachel one of the youngest couples aboard the ironically-named "Modesty of the Seas." They seriously considered having all their remaining meals in their cabin, but the Room Service menu was as severely limited as their cabin space.

Whenever the ship neared port, an announcement was made for everyone to please get clothed, particularly those going ashore. Twenty minutes after departing from each port, the PA system gave the all-clear to revert to the all-together.

While at sea and true to her word, Rachel refused to go completely nude. However, two days into the cruise and after several killer Mojitos poolside, she did go topless. She found it wickedly enjoyable.

About that time, on the sun deck at the stern of the ship far away from Rachel, and after imbibing several strong tropical beverages himself, Fred stripped off his swim trunks and sunbathed face-down on a lounge chair. He fell asleep in that position; the resulting sunburn transformed his stark-white posterior into blazing red hillocks. Meals and morning constitutionals were extremely uncomfortable for the rest of the voyage.

All that week, Fred and Rachel saw things that were never meant to be seen. They particularly avoided being in the vicinity of shipboard athletic events like ping pong, tennis, yoga, and aerobics. A "Caribbean Night" limbo contest sent them scurrying to a dark bar on the opposite side of the ship.

Rachel knew she'd be spending the next several years in therapy.

The cruise had two formal dinners. When Rachel and Fred arrived suitably gowned and tuxedoed, they saw the males wearing crisp bow ties and the females sporting elegant necklaces - and nothing else.

The last day of the cruise, the pot for the afternoon bingo game stood at $3,500. Rachel, who loved bingo, dragged Fred, who didn't, to the final game to help her with her multiple cards. With the exception of the crew, they were the only ones clothed in the cavernous auditorium.

A sixtysomething 300-pound woman, over six feet tall, sitting next to Fred won the pot. She leaped to her feet, screaming joyfully. Ecstatic, she turned and bear-hugged the first person she could lay hands on, a poor unfortunate soul just rising to his feet.

Fred.

Our hero suddenly found himself enveloped in 300 pounds of soft, undulating flesh. Fred's entire face was smothered into her ample bosom, and something jabbed into his left eye. His protests were completely muffled. Arms pined, his struggles against the bear hug were futile.

Rachel, laughing uncontrollably, was no help at all. She wondered: *Would this be considered attempted murder or sexual assault?*

Finally released, Fred collapsed back onto his seat, gasping for air. As the sight returned to his left eye, he saw his tormentor dancing and jumping all the way down the aisle toward the stage, to claim her prize. To Fred's oxygen-starved brain, it seemed like she was running in slow-motion, in a ghastly *au naturel* parody of the running scene in *Chariots of Fire*, as the theme from that movie played in his head.

Arms spread wide, the woman aimed straight for the bingo caller, the Cruise Director. Having seen what just happened to Fred, he thrust his microphone at his five-foot-two-inch Filipino assistant and fled.

The assistant's scream of terror was abruptly cut short as the naked pink mountain on two legs engulfed him like an octopus shrouding its prey. He disappeared except for his feet, which played a desperate tatoo on the stage.

Upon returning home, Rachel resolved to make all their future travel arrangements herself, while Fred cancelled his subscription to *Playboy* and joined Rachel in therapy.

This story, like most of the Fred stories, is based on true events. The horror, the horror ...

Fred Goes Houseboating

Rachel decided one year that they should take a houseboating vacation. It was something they'd never done and it looked like fun. Besides, she felt they should give the airlines some "cooling off" time, considering several carriers had placed Fred, the World's Worst Tourist, on their No Fly list.

She booked a week's sojourn with a company that rented houseboats to tour the Trent-Severn Waterway system, a delightful picturesque series of lakes, locks and canals northeast of Toronto that stretches 386 km from Georgian Bay in the west to Lake Ontario's Bay of Quinte in the east, operated by Parks Canada as a National Historic Site. Neither she nor Fred had ever captained a houseboat before, but the rental agency assured her that it was easy and that they'd receive instructions before their departure.

Such instructions typically lasted about an hour, including ten minutes spent reviewing a Rental Safety Checklist which, in lieu of the Pleasure Craft Operator Card that all boaters must carry by federal law, allowed them to pilot a powered vessel. Thanks to Fred, their session lasted three hours and resulted in several near-misses with berthed yachts in the marina's capacious harbour as Fred tried to control their ungainly 40-foot houseboat (actually 44 feet long, from pontoon tip to stubby stem). They were finally allowed to depart, and as their unattractive boxy craft chugged slowly out into the lake, their instructor announced he was quitting, effective immediately.

(Rachel had actually booked a 32-foot houseboat, a more manageable size for two people. However, upon arrival at the marina, the engine on their craft refused to start, no matter how much the mechanic cursed it. There was no other 32-footer available, so the agency gave them a much larger 40-footer at the same price. Rachel commented that it seemed a lot of boat for two people to handle, but Fred, happy to get a much roomier vessel, overrode her. He still spent almost an hour on their first night calculating how much more in gas it would cost to operate the craft, compared to what they would have spent with the smaller boat. Upon their return, he intended to demand a credit from the rental agency for the extra cost.)

Things went kinda well for the first two days. They motored down several of the wide Kawartha Lakes, plowing through the waves at a sedate pace. (Fred was quite annoyed to discover their houseboat was incapable of anything remotely resembling high speed; paddling ducks seemed to pass them with ease.) He hogged the helm, located just inside the cabin at the front of the boat, refusing to share captain's duties. Rachel, irritated at being relegated to navigator, nonetheless ably used the charts that came with the boat to keep them on course.

For two nights, they anchored near shore at dusk and enjoyed cosy meals on the front verandah watching the sun set. Each morning, they awoke to find that their anchor had dragged and they had run aground, once on the manicured lawn of a large estate and the second time on some rocks. Both times, they managed to refloat themselves with much revving of the engine, assisted by Fred's pushing and swearing in waist-deep water.

On Day Three, they encountered their first lock.

The many locks of the Trent-Severn Waterway, over 40 in all including the world's highest operating hydraulic lift lock in Peterborough, were built over 100 years ago, and had stoically endured decades of pleasure boaters, underfunded government maintenance, and all kinds of weather.

Then came Fred.

Experienced boaters tense up whenever a houseboat approaches a lock. Lockmasters take their blood pressure pills. They know that most houseboats are rented by folks with little or no boating experience, and that the large boxes on pontoons are notoriously hard to maneuver, especially if it's windy, since the house part of the boat acts as a big sail.

Making his approach, Cap'n Fred saw a narrow channel to the left and a wide expanse of water to the right. Unsure of exactly where the lock was, he steered to the right. It was also the path of least resistance; the wind, blowing briskly, insisted on pushing them to the right anyway.

Right towards the lip of a large dam, over which torrents of excess water cascaded.

A voice blared from a loudspeaker: "Houseboat! That is *not* the lock! You are approaching a dam! Reverse course!"

Fred desperately spun the helm around and gunned the motor. The wind, hitting the side of their floating cottage broadside, had other ideas. It pushed them inexorably towards the edge of the dam. Fishermen in small boats anchored near the dam, quickly hauled in their lines and moved their boats well away from the oncoming behemoth. Some shook their fists, shouting their opinions of houseboating tourists.

Panicked, Fred spun the wheel in the other direction, which succeeded in turning their boat around. He motored away from the dam at the highest speed the engine could muster. Once a safe distance away, he angled to the left, aiming for the narrow channel, hugging the lee shore so close that he risked pranging the prop on the bottom, and cursing the wind that threatened to again push them towards the dam.

They eventually made it inside the channel. "Whew, that was scary," said Rachel.

"Yeah, it's damn hard to control this tub against the wind," muttered Fred, sweating profusely. "And why don't they have a big sign with an arrow showing where the lock is?"

Why didn't you watch where the other boaters were going? thought his crew, somewhat mutinously.

But their fun was just beginning.

Rounding a bend in the channel, they came in sight of the lock. Rachel stood on the front verandah, holding the forward mooring line as they approached the blue line painted on the concrete wharf leading to the closed lock. This was the waiting area, where vessels tied up until the lock doors opened to receive them.

The lock loudspeaker blared: "Ahoy approaching houseboat with the red stripe. Throttle back. You're coming in too fast."

Fred assumed the message was directed at another houseboat and did nothing. (He was, in fact, the only houseboat on approach.)

"Red stripe houseboat! Slow down!" barked the loudspeaker.

Rachel stuck her head into the cabin. "He's talking to you, idiot!"

Fred eased back on the throttle. But the sheer mass of the houseboat, once propelled in a direction, required considerable time and distance to change course.

"Put your engine into full reverse!" yelled the lockmaster over the loudspeaker.

Fred did so, hearing their motor growl far behind him in response. Several onlookers ran to fend off the massive boat as it swept into the wharf. It still hit with a jarring crunch.

Rachel staggered backwards, then threw her mooring line to an onlooker, who passed it around a thick mooring post and flung the end back to Rachel. She grabbed it.

About four feet of water separated the stern from the concrete. The wind caught the boat and pushed the stern farther away from the wall, towards the boats moored on the other side of the canal. Their already-nervous occupants grabbed paddles and poles to fend off the hulking barge approaching them.

The lockmaster bellowed: "Turn your wheel hard away from the wall and throttle forward slowly!"

Turning the wheel away from the wall made no sense to Fred, as he wanted to go *towards* the wall, to tie up his stern line. Quickly concluding that the lockmaster had blurted out the wrong thing in panic, Fred did the opposite, turning the wheel toward the wall while advancing the throttle.

The long houseboat promptly went perpendicular to the canal, effectively blocking all boat traffic. Those boaters not fearfully shouting and brandishing their paddles 'n' poles, shook their heads and laughed. Rachel gave a little moan of mortified despair.

Muttering an oath that was not in the Parks Canada customer service manual, the lockmaster abandoned his station and ran to the hapless houseboat. He leapt aboard, shouldered Fred away from the helm, and spun the wheel around.

"Keep a tight grip on your line!" he ordered Rachel. He gunned the motor and the floating box slowly, ponderously, swung back against the wind towards the wall, with Rachel's line acting as a fulcrum. Another Parks Canada employee snugged the stern line around a stanchion as the stern kissed the wall. The lockmaster killed the engine and gave Fred a stern admonition to pay attention and listen better next time.

About five minutes later, the thick, heavy lock doors swung open, allowing its contents, a motley collection of pleasure boats, to exit. Once the lock was empty, the lockmaster directed the boats waiting on the blue line on the other side of the canal, to enter and slip their lines around the vertical mooring cables spaced 15 feet apart along one side of the cavernous lock.

Then he directed Fred and Rachel to exit their boat and walk it into the lock on their side. They did so, Fred miffed at not being allowed to drive it in and the boaters already in the lock heaving sighs of relief. Our heroes halted their craft just before the closed doors at the other end.

"Now pass your mooring lines around the cables near the fore and aft of your boat and climb back aboard. *Do NOT* tie your lines to the cables! Hold them and let them slip downwards as the water level in the lock lowers."

The entrance doors clanged shut, then the water level slowly lowered, dropping the encased boats to the level of the lower lake. Once there, the doors facing them opened. The lockmaster directed the boats on the opposite side to exit first, which they gratefully did, glad to be away from the incompetent skipper of the houseboat. Then he ordered Fred to *slowly* drive his boat forward out of the lock.

Rachel, standing aft, cast off her mooring line. Fred, at the bow, released his line and ran into the cabin to start the motor. He advanced the throttle as directed and their big box started forward. Outside the lock, a double line of boats were tied up along either side of the canal, awaiting their turn to lock through. When they caught sight of the lumbering houseboat coming at them, crews grabbed paddles and poles and positioned themselves along their gunwales, just in case.

Way too slow, thought Cap'n Fred, and eased the throttle forward.

"Too fast! Throttle back!" commanded the lockmaster over the loudspeaker.

Already halfway down the canal, Fred saw no reason to go slower. In fact, as he cleared the last moored boat, a beautiful 45-foot luxury cabin cruiser made by Carver (the Rolls Royce of boats), and spied the open lake beyond, he gunned the throttle and spun his wheel, steering for open water.

Fred forgot that he still had 36 feet of houseboat behind him. The first eight feet may have cleared the moored boats, but the rest of the massive boat was still very much within the narrow canal.

"STOP!" screamed the lockmaster, but it was too late.

The stern of the houseboat swung in a wide arc as the behemoth responded to its new direction and speed. It hit the side of the tall, stately cabin cruiser and scraped along as the houseboat's speed increased. The rear corner of the houseboat's upper deck caught on something on the cabin cruiser's side and, acting like a gigantic can opener, peeled a four-foot long, foot-wide strip of fibreglass off the gleaming Carver.

The houseboat chugged away, the strip of fibreglass dangling from its upper deck like an obscene pennant.

Fred either didn't hear, or chose to ignore, the angry shouts in his wake, which included bellows from the loudspeaker to heave to. Rachel stood frozen, dumbfounded, gawking at the ugly scar on the boat behind them.

Several small boats bravely positioned themselves in Fred's path, forcing him to stop and kill his engine. Rachel flung out the anchor and there they bobbed until an OPP Marine Unit cruiser arrived.

To say that the Carver's owner, an American tourist exploring the waterway he'd heard so much about, was furious, would be like saying the eruption of Mt. Vesuvius was a hiccup. Among his more printable comments, was a vow to lobby Congress to force

Canada to reinstate the death penalty.

Insurance particulars were exchanged under the watchful eye of the OPP officer, who warned Fred that he could also be charged with careless driving. He allowed them to continue their houseboat vacation, with the strict proviso that Rachel manned the helm from now on.

Their subsequent passage through the remaining locks on their journey went without a hitch under the sure hand of Captain Rachel. They discovered that the lockmaster at their first lock, where they had the accident, had called his counterparts to warn them about the Red Stripe houseboat traversing the system. So they were treated warily, with kid gloves, by nervous lock staff on high alert. Sometimes, they were the only boat placed inside a lock, the other boats kept out for their own safety.

The weather was perfect as they motored through the sparkling lakes between locks: blue skies, calm waters, hot temperatures tempered by fair breezes. They took to anchoring in mid-day, to swim around the boat and then climb the narrow ladder bolted to the rear wall of the dwelling to sunbathe on the flat roof, high above the water, sipping chilled white wine.

Anchored in the middle of a lake on one such afternoon, Rachel, encouraged by her husband and several glasses of wine, undid her bikini bra and sunbathed topless. Fred had reminded her that it was quite legal to do so in Ontario and besides, no one could see her lying flat up there.

She luxuriated in the warm sun caressing her body, the gentle swaying of the boat, the soothing peace of the lake. Suddenly a powerful cigarette boat thundered by, one of those vessels composed of 90% unmuffled V8 engine, 10% cockpit, and 0% brains behind the wheel. The long, lean boat passed so close that its massive wake sent their vessel rocking crazily. Forgetting her state of undress, she sat up and shook her fist at the young men in the offending boat, who hooted and whistled their pleasure at what they saw. She looked down, gave a startled "Aack!," and grabbed her towel.

Fred, meanwhile, had fallen asleep. The abrupt oscillations of their houseboat sent him rotating like a log towards the edge of the roof deck, where he banged into the safety rail. He awoke with a start, just as the rocking sent him rolling back towards Rachel. As he thumped into her, she smacked him hard on his butt with one hand, her other hand clutching the towel over her chest.

"Wha ... what made the boat rock so badly?" Fred stammered. "And why did you just whack me?"

"We were buzzed by a powerboat on steroids, and I hit you 'cause you talked me into sunbathing topless. Those guys in the powerboat just got an eyeful of these!" she said as she dropped the towel to reveal the Twins in all their glory.

"Woo-HOO!" came a shout from the water. Startled, Rachel and Fred looked out over their port side. A pair of canoeists were paddling by; a middle-aged couple. The male was gawking at Rachel sitting up in full view. The female gave a disgusted snort, then splashed the man with her paddle.

With an astonished squawk, flushing beet red, Rachel hurriedly recovered herself with the towel. Then swatted Fred again.

On their second-to-last day, en route back to the marina, with Fred still serving as frustrated navigator, he sent them down the wrong lake, leading them to a weedy dead-end instead of the expected channel. Their propeller became hopelessly fouled. Under the strain of trying to spin while jammed with aquatic flora, the engine gave a funny *ker-clunk* and stopped. They were able to restart the motor, but the prop refused to spin.

Rachel called the rental agency on her cell phone and a rescue boat eventually arrived. Despite much tinkering and swearing, the mechanic couldn't fix the drive train. So they had to endure a long, slow, ignominious tow all the way back to the marina.

"A perfect end to yet another perfect vacation," Rachel muttered.

It was their first, last, and only houseboating holiday.

.

Happily, the historic Trent-Severn Waterway still endures.

Fred vs. Gorgonzola,
King of the Monsters

Rachel once had the opportunity to travel to Japan on business. Her boss suggested her husband accompany her, and in a massive lapse of judgement, she invited him.

So that's how Rachel found herself at 38,000 feet winging westward over the Pacific with Fred, the Black Sheep of tourists.

By the time the 13 hour flight ended, Fred had alienated the smiling, extremely-polite JAL flight attendants, one of whom devoutly wished she had her honoured grandfather's antique samurai sword with her.

They stayed at a Western-style hotel in Tokyo, with Western-style bathrooms and Western-style food, which was fine by Fred, a traveller who demanded the sameness of home in foreign lands.

One day, Rachel's Japanese client, Yoshi, invited them to dinner with his wife at their home. Rachel drilled Fred in basic Japanese customs and he promised to be on his best behavior.

Though Rachel was as nervous as a comedian at a city budget meeting, the evening started well. Fred left his shoes outside the entrance, bowed deeply upon meeting his hosts, only grunted once as he knelt on his cushion for pre-dinner drinks, and accepted a small cup of warm sake with grace, sipping it without grimacing too much at the taste.

Several cups in, the talk turned to movies, and Fred declared his affection for that famous Japanese scaly green sea monster with radioactive fire-breath and a penchant for trashing Tokyo.

"Ah, Gojira!" said Yoshi, beaming. "King of the Monsters."

"Eh? We call him Gorgonzola," said Fred.

"Gorgonzola?" repeated Yoshi slowly. "Isn't that a cheese? I believe in your language, Gojira means Godzilla."

"No, no, trust me, it's Gorgonzola," said Fred with the authority of someone who never lets facts clutter his mind.

Rachel adroitly steered the conversation onto another topic.

Thankfully, dinner was all Western food, as the hosts wished their foreign guests to feel at home. Everything was cut into bite-sized pieces, including the steak. Fred couldn't master chopsticks to save his life. Since there wasn't any Western cutlery available, he ate with his fingers. Their hosts pretended not to notice.

After dinner, Fred asked to use the bathroom. Closing the sliding washroom door, Fred turned and gaped. Instead of the familiar raised toilet, there was a long, narrow, white porcelain basin sunk in the floor.

Fred deduced that one must squat over the thing, and so he did. At least until his trick knee gave out, at which point it got messy.

Sometime later, after taking an impromptu self-guided tour around the entire house, Fred sauntered back to the others, wearing the comfy slippers someone had thoughtfully placed inside the bathroom door.

Their hosts looked at Fred's feet and gasped in horror. Rachel turned to look and gave an anguished squeak.

Her dodo husband-san had forgotten one of the local customs she had briefed him about.

Japanese walk about their homes on woven tatami mats wearing only socks, except in the bathroom, where one wears the "bathroom slippers," which are then left by the door for the next user. These slippers are *never* worn outside the bathroom.

Fastidious about cleanliness and hygiene, Japanese would be appalled if some idiot wandered around their pristine home wearing such unclean footwear. Fred, Idiot Emeritus, had committed a cultural gaffe on par with offering non-alcoholic beer to an Irishman.

Rachel made profuse apologies, followed later by a substantial gift. The couple grudgingly forgave her for bringing an uncultured barbarian into their home.

(However, Yoshi wished Gojira did exist, so he could emerge, shrieking and flaming, from Lake Ontario and trash Toronto, Fred's hometown. In his sleep, he often dreamt about it, smiling.)

Fred Goes Out for a Sandwich

Rachel entered the staff lunchroom, waving to the three women holding a seat for her at their usual table. After buying a diet pop and a yogurt to go with her brown-bag salad, she joined her lunch hour companions.

"So, Rache, how was your long weekend?" asked Melissa, who worked in Accounting, down the hall from Marketing where Rachel worked. "I know you took last Friday off. Where'd ya go? What'd ya do? Did it liven up your dreary January?"

Rachel snorted and methodically applied dressing to her salad before answering. "Very strange. Fred went out for a sandwich."

"What's so strange about that?" said Amy around a mouthful of her own sandwich. Amy worked in Accounting with Melissa.

Rachel rolled her eyes. "He wanted an authentic Philly Cheesesteak sandwich."

"So? Did you go to some deli around here?" asked Susan, who hung her coat one floor up on the Executive floor, where she was Executive Assistant to one of the corporation's five vice-presidents.

"Nope. Not my Fred," replied Rachel, taking a bite of her salad. "Philadelphia."

"Whaaat? He drove all the way from Toronto to Philadelphia, in the dead of winter, just to get a sandwich?" said Amy, unbelieving.

"No. WE drove all the way to Philadelphia. In MY Smart Car. Fred insisted on taking it because its little three-cylinder diesel engine gets such great mileage. But there was no way I was letting him go all that way in my bright blue pride and joy, so I went along to ensure my car stayed in one piece."

"So, um, knowing that your Fred is the World's Worst Tourist, as you've told us so many times, how'd the trip go?" asked Melissa.

Rachel took another bite of rabbits' delight, chewed, swallowed, and said: "The usual with Fred. We got through the U.S. border without any major incident, though it was a close call. Fred pissed off the customs officer by making what he thought were funny comments about America's massive debt and their screwed-up foreign policy. He finally shut up when I whacked him a good one on the shoulder and the guy let us pass."

"Then what?" said Susan, eyeing a good-looking guy in Sales two tables over, a new hire since just three weeks.

"Well, we drove into Philly and, Fred being Fred, he took a wrong turn off the expressway. While he was blaming me for not being able to read a map properly, we ended up in the wrong part of town. It was a bad place; it looked like a very tough neighbourhood."

Amy had also noticed the good-looking guy. She hiked up the hem of her already-short skirt, revealing a scandalous amount of sleek nylon-clad leg, while adjusting her figure-hugging blouse to display even more cleavage than usual. She caught Susan looking at her, frowning.

"What?" said Amy. "You three are married or in relationships. Me, I'm currently in the market, and I'm just making myself more marketable. So, Rache, what happened next?"

"We ran out of windshield washer fluid. And we couldn't drive without that stuff, because it was below zero, with salted, slushy roads. We didn't have a spare container of washer fluid - the car's tiny trunk, in the rear just above the tiny engine, barely accommodated our overnight bags. So we pulled into a convenience store - with more bars on its windows and doors than a jail - in this creepy neighbourhood to buy some fluid and that's when everything went to hell."

"Just adding windshield washer fluid? Huh, even *I* know how to do that," snorted Melissa.

"YOU don't drive a Smart Car, being operated by someone who certainly doesn't qualify as smart," retorted Rachel. She sighed the sigh of the long-suffering. "The thing to know about Smart Cars, girls, is that nothing's smart about them. They're actually Dumb

Cars; extremely difficult to service. Fred and I both went into the store. I had the owner's manual; we needed it to figure out how to fill the washer fluid tank. I didn't even know where it was! I've never had to fill it; my dealer usually tops up all my fluids for me when I come in for service.

"Anyway, while Fred bought some fluid, I found out where to put it. You have to open the narrow grill just below the windshield outside on the driver's side. You use your key to open the lock holding the grill closed. Once the grill is open, you fish out a small hose thingy and pour the washer fluid in. We went to pour the stuff in as soon as we left the store. Well, the lock didn't want to open; it was frozen with ice and slushy snow gunk. Fred, having the patience of a three-year-old, jerked and forced the key, trying to get the damn thing to turn in the lock. Guess what?"

"What?" asked Susan.

"The key broke off."

"*Nooo,*" said Melissa and Amy in unison.

Susan shrugged. "So you simply used your own key to start your car and get out of that bad neighbourhood, right?"

"That WAS my key. I only have one spare, and it was at home."

"*Ohhh,*" said Melissa and Amy, still in unison.

"It gets worse. The curse of Fred was working overtime. When the key broke, he flipped out. Before I could stop him, he threw the key fob onto the icy ground and stomped on it. I yelled that we needed the fob to unlock the car - Smart Car doors don't have key-holes; you lock and unlock the doors electronically with your key fob. Of course, we had locked the doors before going into the store. I grabbed the fob from the ground before he could stomp it again, but it was too late. It wouldn't unlock the doors. My temperamental klutz had locked us out of the car!"

"*Geee,*" said Melissa and Amy, going for a Tony Award in unison.

"Will you two STOP that!" snapped Rachel, glaring.

"Well, I assume you just called the local Mercedes-Benz dealer in Philly to come over with a spare key so you could open up and drive your car," said Susan.

Rachel made a funny choking sound. "Yeah, about that: Luckily I had my cell phone in my jacket pocket, because my purse was locked inside the car. So was Fred's cell, along with his wallet and our passports. He had walked into the convenience store with only a five dollar bill; he was worried we might be robbed. Anyway, we called the local dealer. He could do nothing! We discovered that each Smart Car can only be opened and operated by its unique key. There are no 'master keys.' If you ever lose - or break - your keys, you have to order replacements direct from Mercedes-Benz in Germany! That takes weeks!"

"So what did you do?" asked Amy, lusty thoughts of that good-looking guy on hold for the moment.

"Well, it was late afternoon and it was getting dark. We certainly didn't want to be stuck in that neighbourhood after dark. So we called a tow truck. The dealer had warned us to insist that the towing company send us a flat bed truck, because apparently another issue with Smart Cars is that they shouldn't be towed like conventional cars.

"When the tow truck finally arrived - it took forEVER and it was dark by then - it was a normal tow truck. Not a flat bed. I was getting quite panicky and Fred was beyond irritated. He started reaming out the truck driver, who cut him off by insisting he COULD tow Smart Cars. In fact, he claimed he towed them all the time.

"So Fred told the man to go ahead. He hooked up my car, we climbed into the cab with the guy - who was doused in WAY too much cologne - and we got the hell out of there."

"Whew," said Melissa. "All that just for a lousy sandwich."

"Oh, our story's not over yet," said Rachel, spearing the last of her salad with gusto, as if the lettuce represented something else that she really wanted to spear. "We were halfway to the Mercedes dealership, going down a busy street, when my car fell off the hook! There was a sudden loud *BANG* and then, no car! The driver and Fred tried to out-swear each other as he jammed on the brakes and backed up. Luckily, there was no apparent damage to my car.

But we insisted on waiting right there until a flat bed arrived.

"It eventually did - I think Philly only has the one flat bed - and they loaded my car onto it. We finally made it to the dealer, who put the car in his fenced-in secured lot."

"How'd you pay the towing company, if both your wallets were locked inside the car?" asked Susan.

"Well, fortunately I was wearing my Tilley hat - I usually do when we travel - and I always keep money inside the hat, in the concealed pocket in the crown. I had $60 cash in U.S. dollars. The company normally charges more for a tow, but considering how their first driver dropped my car, and how they had originally sent a tow truck when we had specified a flat bed, they accepted the $60."

Rachel started in on her yogurt. She shook her head with a strained laugh; a half-crazy sound with no mirth in it. "But things just kept getting weirder. We needed a place to stay for the night. We caught one break: there was a decent hotel just two blocks from the dealership. Fred boasted that he too took precautions when we travelled. He said he had a hidden credit card in his Tilleys. We both travel in Tilley clothes, all of which come with hidden pockets. I was greatly relieved; I almost kissed the bonehead. We could pay for our room, eat at the hotel restaurant and charge our meals to our room, and buy essential toiletries and some PJs in the hotel gift shop.

"So we walked to the hotel. When we arrived, Fred told me to get a room while he went to the washroom to retrieve his credit card. In our Tilley pants, the hidden pocket is on the inside, so you have to undo your pants to get at it. I told the front desk clerk that my husband would soon return from the men's room with a credit card. 'But our men's room off the lobby is closed for renovations,' said the clerk.

"All of a sudden, there came a tremendous shriek from the ladies' room. A woman ran out, screaming that there was a man, a twisted pervert, standing in middle of their restroom with his pants unbuckled and his hand down inside the front of his underwear, digging away in his private parts!"

The other three women looked at each other, wide-eyed. "Fred," Susan said finally.

"Fred," Rachel sighed. "Seems the hidden pocket that he referred to in his Tilleys, was the secret pocket in his Tilley travel *underwear*, which is located in the, um, front pouch. It looks quite suggestive, to put it mildly, to retrieve anything inside it. Fred went into the ladies' room when he found the men's room closed, and thought he was alone. Which he was, until that woman entered. The impatient fool never thought to use a stall."

Amy looked at Melissa, who looked at Susan, who looked at Amy. All three dissolved into hysterical laughter.

"S-sorry, Rache," gasped Melissa finally. "It's just the mental picture of your Fred groping away down there and some poor woman walks in on him!"

"And, and what a RIDICULOUS place to hide a credit card!" wheezed Susan, fighting for air.

Rachel sighed. "Thanks, girls. Appreciate your sympathy. Well, we eventually got everyone calmed down - the front desk clerk paged the manager and was dialling the police when I convinced her to put the phone down - and Fred emerged, fully dressed, proclaiming he wasn't a pervert. He told them what he had been doing. The lady slapped his face and stormed out of the hotel. The desk clerk refused to touch the credit card. Understandable, considering where it came from. She made Fred wipe it with sanitizer, then swipe it himself through the card terminal. We *finally* got a room key.

"After buying some essentials - I now own a nightie with 'Fabulous Philly' across the chest in big neon pink letters - we went up to our room. We were still at square one. We had no way of unlocking the car or getting it going. While Fred was ranting and raving about the dealer's failure to help us, I had an idea. I called my dad. He drove to our house, and got in with the spare key we keep hidden outside."

"Oh, lemme guess," interrupted Amy. "In a fake rock that looks *so* obvious, it's the first place burglars look."

Rachel fixed her with a look. "No, honey. You forget who I'm married to. Fred thought up a much more inventive hiding place. It's in one of our garden gnomes that we leave out year-round, a cute little dwarf."

"And it's under his cute little dwarf boot," Amy chirped.

"No. It's up his ass."

The women laughed. Rachel went on: "So Dad got my spare Smart Car key - I told him where I kept it - and drove to the FedEx counter at Pearson Airport late Friday night and sent it by special overnight courier to our hotel in Philadelphia. We were surcharged a fortune for the overnight delivery.

"Once we had the spare key, we used its fob to unlock the doors, then drove to the restaurant Fred had found on the Internet, where he finally had his damn authentic Philly Cheesesteak sandwich. Then we drove home."

The other women shook their heads.

"Some weekend," said Melissa.

"What a bloody hassle just to get a stupid sandwich," said Susan.

"Yeah," said Rachel. "And do you know what that stupid sandwich cost us? With the towing, the hotel room, meals, the FedEx special delivery, and so on? Six. Hundred. Dollars."

"Unreal," said Amy, as the others shook their heads again. There was a long sympathetic pause. Then Melissa said:

"Rache, next time I ask how your weekend went, please don't tell us."

Susan asked: "Why do you stay married to that - please pardon my French - *schmuck*?"

Rachel chuckled. "I often ask myself that, usually just after one of our trips together. I've narrowed it down to three very good reasons: One, he works for the government, so we get amazing health benefits. Two, he makes me laugh. Most times not intentionally, but he does make me laugh. And lastly, but certainly not leastly: for the same reason Marge Simpson stays married to that oaf, Homer."

"What's that?" asked Susan, who was much too level-headed and career-focused to even consider watching *The Simpsons*.

"The sex. He gives great sex."

Amy finally did get a date with that good-looking guy in Sales and they are currently living together. They share a mutual love of gourmet cooking, classic Disney movies, and Lego bricks.

Melissa discovered her husband was cheating on her, hired a pit bull of a divorce lawyer who took him to the cleaners, and is now a contented single mom to her two daughters. She delights in driving her girls to soccer games and gymnastics practice in her ex's beautifully-restored cherry red 1926 Lincoln "L" convertible touring sedan.

Susan achieved her Masters in Business Administration and got promoted to Vice-President when her boss, the former V-P, got caught embezzling funds. She still doesn't watch **The Simpsons.**

Rachel won two awards for her marketing campaigns, got promoted to Director of Marketing and, to the utter astonishment of her colleagues, is still married to the World's Worst Tourist.

"To travel hopefully is a better thing than to arrive."

– Robert Louis Stevenson

Epilogue

The Canada Customs Inspector glanced at the man waiting at the red line in the international arrivals area of Toronto's Lester B. Pearson International Airport. Thin, young, Asian, nervous.

Hmmm, this next one might be interesting, thought Ted.

He finished the formalities with the family of three in front of him, welcoming them back to Canada as he returned their passports. *Nice family, mother and son in particular. I wonder about that bald-headed father, though. Guy his age, 58, and they're returning from a huge comic book convention in San Diego that HE wanted to attend. Weird. Wonder if he's wearing Batman underwear?*

Ted beckoned to the Asian man to approach his kiosk.

The man seemed to be in his late twenties. His nervousness was palpable as he stood before the Customs Inspector.

"Where are you arriving from?" asked Ted, as he took the man's passport, noting it was a Canadian passport.

"Shanghai," he replied with a tremulous smile. "But I'm Canadian citizen, returning home from visiting parents in Shanghai." He had a thick accent.

"Uh-huh," said Ted noncommittally. He flipped open the passport. It felt and looked authentic, but something seemed wrong. Was there something "off" about the man's photo? He passed the document through his scanner.

The Customs Inspector leaned back in his chair and fixed the man with a steady gaze. "Where do you live?"

"Gelp," replied the man, eyes downcast.

"Gelp? I've never heard of Gelp," said Ted.

"Oh, is in Canada, yes sir."

"Really?"

"Near Niagara Falls," the man added helpfully. "Beautiful Niagara Falls."

"I've never heard of Gelp," Ted repeated. "And I see that the handwritten address in your passport states Toronto."

"I ... I just move. Very recently. To Gelp." The man, his face now perspiring noticeably, dug out a piece of paper from his pocket and presented it to the Customs Inspector. There was an address printed in block letters on the paper. "See? Gelp."

Ted looked at the paper. The address was for Guelph. The guy had no idea how to pronounce it, obviously having never been there. Suspicions fully aroused, Ted escorted the man to the Immigration officers for further questioning.

Hours later, at the end of his shift, Ted walked into Immigration and asked what had become of that Asian man.

"You were right to be suspicious of him, Ted," said an Immigration officer. "After some intensive grilling, er, questioning, the man broke down and admitted that he was trying to enter Canada illegally. He'd bought a stolen Canadian passport in Shanghai, that had been swiped from a careless Canadian tourist within the past 36 hours, and was quickly and somewhat-professionally altered."

"Gelp indeed," said Ted. "Did you find out whose passport it actually belonged to?"

"Some guy named Fred."

"So this Fred guy is now stuck in communist China with no passport. Huh. Bet he's having fun right now."

Book Two:
Humour on Wry, with Mayo

"Don't Let the Bed Bugs Bite"

My friend Bob retired early from teaching high school and now manages a movie theatre in a Big City. Several years ago, the local TV station, always seeking sensationalism, decided to host a panel of experts on "the growing bed bug epidemic." (Two infestations one year, three the next = one epidemic.)

Their researcher discovered that bed bugs can infest many places: nursing homes, cruise ships, hotels, college dorms, homes, and movie theatres. To speak for the latter, they invited Bob to the panel. Since its regularly-scheduled, heavily-hyped comedy show had been abruptly cancelled, due to its star slipping yet again into rehab, the national network had picked up the bed bug show and would broadcast it live across Canada.

Bob had grudgingly surrendered to youth the things that are youth, including his hair. The makeup lady quailed when he walked into the studio. She applied two different powders, but Bob's chrome dome still gave off a blinding glare under the bright spotlights.

She rummaged deep in her bag and extracted a very small tube of a very expensive anti-glare gel. Bob's head took the entire tube. That blew her makeup budget for the month.

Bob's fellow panellists were the vice-president of a pest control company and a professor of entomology. The prof had brought along a sealed vial containing dozens of live and hungry bed bugs. The producer was overcome with joy, but the rest of the TV crew and Gloria, the carefully-coiffed bottle-blonde on-air host, exchanged nervous glances.

The show's theme music sounded, Gloria mangled the introductions, and the panel got underway. Everything went well, until the professor suggested letting a bed bug dine on the arm of the V-P, who had to agree, to preserve his macho image. The producer gleefully ordered a cameraperson to get a close up of the feeding. Gloria squirmed in her chair, barely hiding her revulsion.

The bug was extracted, placed on the victim's arm, and promptly began to gorge. The prof placed the resealed vial with the rest of the colony on the table between him and Bob, and everyone watched the feasting insect.

Gloria asked Bob about the (admittedly rare) occurrence of bed bugs in theatres and he launched into his reply with gusto. Because of his years of teaching, Bob talked with his hands.

One of his sweeping gesticulations connected with the vial, sending it flying off the table. Bob made a futile grab for it as it arced through the air. Gloria's perfectly-lipsticked mouth was just forming a shocked "O" when the glass shattered on the hard floor.

Gloria uttered an unearthly shriek and launched straight up from her chair. She hit the ground running, heading for the studio door. She would have made it too, except she forgot she was "miked." The cord attached to the microphone attached to her jacket snapped taunt before she had taken three steps. She was yanked backward, her feet flew out from under her, and she crashed to the floor. The same floor now crawling with bed bugs.

Anyone impressed by her first shriek were positively astonished with her second one. Though the studio was soundproofed, people heard it two floors down.

One dedicated cameraperson filmed the whole thing, broadcasting it live, nationwide.

Apart from the area lit by spotlights, TV studios during a show are dark places, full of cracks and crevices. Bed bugs love the dark and live in cracks and crevices, which is what the colony scurried into posthaste.

Everyone fled the studio, with the pest control V-P yelling into his cell phone that he had a Code Red - major infestation - requiring room quarantine and an extermination team IMMEDIATELY.

The insect was still on his arm.

Although this story is partially fictional, I still sleep fitfully.

Hell's Bell

Innkeepers deal with many trials and tribulations on a daily basis, like the following true story:

The opening white pages in Ma Bell's phone book boldly proclaim: "Our customers come first. We are here to help you."

Naively believing that, a motel operator in Southwestern Ontario calls Ma's Customer Service. After waiting on hold for an eternity ("Your call is important to us"), the line goes dead. She tries again. And again. After each eternal wait, she gets disconnected. Finally, she reaches an actual live person (obviously a major technical glitch). She explains her problem:

The motel has five phone lines. Bell's bills charge them for six lines. The innkeeper had recently discovered that line four has two phone numbers on it.

This situation has existed since Bell installed her new phone system four years ago. Bell has no idea how it happened. She requests a reimbursement for the phantom sixth line. The Bell rep says they can only reimburse for problems that happened within the past three months, "because we don't have records on when your account started."

The innkeeper is incredulous that Canada's largest, oldest, stodgiest phone company doesn't keep records that far back. (She is required to keep her motel's records for seven years.) She's somewhat mollified when the rep pledges to cancel one of the dual numbers on line four.

The next day, line four goes dead.

From another line, she calls both line four numbers. One is no longer in service, the other is now for outgoing calls only.

She calls Bell. After first trying to blame her phone system (which they installed), the rep promises to have line four up and running by tomorrow.

Next morning, the motel's main line, the only number in the phone book and in all their advertising, goes dead. But line four is active again, as promised.

The harried innkeeper, now alternating between contemplating suicide or bloody murder, calls Bell. She's transferred to someone with a Ph.D. in Obscure Explanations, who speaks 300 words a minute. As if she's a seasoned phone technician, he describes how she can fix the problem herself. Twenty seconds in, the innkeeper's eyes glaze over and her blood pressure redlines.

He finally says Bell will fix her main line by late afternoon.

4:00 p.m. Main line still comatose. Innkeeper visits backyard shed, retrieves axe. Calls Bell. Yells a lot. Bell promises a solution "very shortly."

Dinnertime. Main line still catatonic. But Bell has indeed been busy: line four now deceased again and the other three lines cannot receive incoming calls. In the world of telephony, her motel has now ceased to exist.

Bell Customer Service receives a somewhat agitated call from the innkeeper. Eventually transferred to a manager (probably because the Suicide Hotline was busy), she's assured she'll receive Priority Service - first thing next morning.

Innkeeper starts sharpening axe on a whetstone, while sweetly informing manager that her motel relies on the phone for 80% of its business, she pays Bell $500 a month for their "service," so waiting until tomorrow is unacceptable. Manager sympathizes, but that's the best he can do.

Innkeeper calls Bell's Executive Office. Closed for the day.

She calls again next morning. Talks to a very nice man with a wonderful voice who listens and completely understands why she's upset and would like to rectify the situation by talking about her long distance bill and the great deals available from Bell.

She hangs up. Reaches for axe. Husband has hidden it.

Since then, she has switched phone companies; laughs uncontrollably whenever she hears the words "customer service"; and teaches her kids that being the biggest does not necessarily mean being the best.

In life, I too am frequently disconnected.

Costco Customs

Like thousands of fellow Peterburgers, within days of its opening, my family and I visited Peterborough's new Costco discount warehouse, otherwise known as "the store with products of ginormous size" (like a box of batteries that would power every toy in an entire neighbourhood, or a package of hot dogs that would gorge a scout troop).

Wandering around that cavernous establishment, awe-struck at the sheer massiveness of all the stuff, I've observed that Costco is changing the behaviors of some local townspeople.

For example, Costco graciously and generously provides a host of food-tasting stations. While their commercial motive is to encourage people to buy the goodies they're sampling (and I can personally attest it works, too), there has been an unexpected side effect: It's reawakened our ancient, long-dormant tribal grazing habits.

Flocks of folks migrate from one station to another, sampling the tantalizing foods and drinks, while keeping a wary eye out for predators anxious to butt in line to snatch a morsel.

It's like watching animal herds on the Serengeti, but without the safari vehicles full of camera-faced tourists. The Discovery Channel should get a film crew down here to record this phenomena. Would be a lot cheaper than flying to Africa. And you wouldn't have to feed the crew, either.

Another behavior modification: For our teens and twentysomethings, going to Costco has become the ultimate cheap date. Couples walk hand-in-hand through the place, stopping to nibble at one food station after another, while murmuring sweet endearments to each other ("honey, are you gonna finish that crepe-wrapped ham-and-cheese thingy, or shall I grab another for myself?" "Oh look, darling: cappuccino.").

Finally, their bellies full and the patience of the food servers exhausted (going back for seconds is frowned upon), the couple buys the latest bargain-priced DVD and returns home. Dinner and a movie, Costco style.

Young men who really want to impress their dates only use the food stations as appetizers, before elegantly escorting their honeys to the snack bar for Costco's famous all-beef $2 hot dog-with-a-pop special. If they really want to splurge, they spring for pizza slices, or ribs, or even Montreal smoked meat.

Actually, it's not just dating couples that do this. Since Costco has come to town, whenever my wife offers to treat me to lunch, she first checks the change bin in her car for toonies and loonies. Nothing but the best for me.

Having a place like Costco also means folks can go on healthy walks year-round in a safe, well-lit, climate-controlled environment. You see so many people doing it: trudging up and down the miles of aisles, from one side of the huge store to the other. Sometimes twice.

And they get added exercise by pushing an enormous shopping cart which, the more they walk, the heavier and heavier it gets as more big-bulk items get piled into it. The result: a combined aerobics and weight-resistance workout. Cardio-shopping! What a health benefit! Why hasn't Oprah talked about this?

The workout experience can be further enhanced if one tries out the various exercise machines offered for sale throughout the store. (But it's recommended that you buy the colourful fleece workout clothing first, before donning it to exercise. Or at least leave the tags attached, for easy scanning on check-out.)

I've observed that, unlike the latest fad diets, the Costco workout regimen actually results in guaranteed weight-loss, every time you do it.

It occurs right after you visit the friendly cashier, and especially affects the cash in your wallet.

My Costco membership was revoked due to excessive over-sampling.

4th Down, Bases Loaded, Who's Got the Puck?

I'm about to make a startling revelation, at great personal risk, considering I live in a rabid hockey town that gets fanatical about other sports to kill time during hockey's off-season. Here goes:

Not all males are into sports.

Shocking, but true. Some men, outwardly normal and productive members of society, don't know a Maple Leaf from a Blue Jay, an Argonaut from an astronaut, a tee time from a tea time.

They manage to blithely go through life without knowing the latest scores, detailed sports statistics, histories of the hottest multi-millionaire athletes, best draft picks, and the top 10 reasons why every city desperately needs a new billion-dollar arena or else society will crumble.

These are the men who constantly embarrass themselves when invited to parties to watch The Big Game on TV, to cheer their team to victory (because without such lusty encouragement, said team would surely lose). These woeful males enjoy the camaraderie, the cold beer, the hot snacks, but always cause their friends' eyes to roll upwards accompanied by agonized groans when they ask:

"So, d'ya think the Leafs will make that winning home run today?"

And it's a Grey Cup party.

(At a Stanley Cup party, they naively inquire if the Tiger Cats will make a hole in one.)

These guys are not deliberately trying to be funny, or disrupt the convivial gathering. They really, truly don't know anything about organized sports.

While psychologists debate the reasons for this aberrant behavior, and drug companies develop expensive pharmaceuticals to correct it, to me, the answer is simple:

Their brains aren't wired for it.

It's all about genetics. Most males are born with an ability to play, watch and understand sports. It's as natural as shrieking obscenities at clued-out referees and umpires.Other males happily spend countless hours on wasteful non-sports pursuits like creating symphonies, painting pictures, writing books, gourmet cooking, and - most useless of all - gardening. Giving such men a subscription to *Sports Illustrated* would be as effective as teaching kids how to spell phonetically. (Although *Sports Illustrated*'s annual swimsuit issue has universal appeal.)

Enthusiasm for sports is derived from the same gene that compels men to tinker with car engines, mangle home renovations, and hunt wildlife. While others, absent that gene, wonder what all the fuss is about.

It's a left side, right side of the brain thing.

But it's nothing to be ashamed about. In our great multi-cultural society, surely there is room for non-sports men? Today, as we embrace diversity and the differently-abled, can we not also accept those who can't tell a yard line from a blue line?

It takes all types to make a world. Unsportsmanlike males have secretly been part of our civilization for millennia, since cavepersons started flinging rocks at each other and calling it football. Some of them have even managed to make positive contributions to society.

Gays, lesbians, bisexuals and hopelessly-confuseds have come out of their closets, so isn't it time for sports-challenged males to emerge from their dugouts, to stand proudly in the sunshine alongside sweaty jocks and their moist fans?

And when you invite such men over to watch the game on TV, don't laugh when they ask "who's on first?" and it's a hockey game. They are not stupid. Just different.

Now please pardon me. I've been invited to a Jays game with my buddies, and I must read up on their star quarterback so I don't look foolish. I think they have a good shot at winning the Masters this year.

I always have trouble keeping score.

Going Postal

The following tale is all-too-true.

Friends of ours bought a house in a new development in Milton. As such, their mail "service" was a large bank of "super mailboxes" at the end of their street. This meant that homeowners had to slog through rain, sleet, snow, ice and hail to get their mail. (The former mantra of mail carriers has been adroitly foisted onto the public, resulting in diminished service which, of course, necessitates postal rate hikes each January.) Two weeks after taking possession of their new home, Doug and Shelina (not their real names) trekked to the post office to obtain a key for their mailbox, so they could start getting their mail delivered there. Upon hearing they were new owners, the Canada Post counter clerk shifted into "special customer service" mode.

"Drivers licence," demanded the clerk. Shelina produced hers. "This is not your new address, is it?" the clerk smirked, batting a wisp of hair away from her eyes.

"No, we just moved," said Shelina.

Smiling like Sylvester ogling Tweety, the clerk said nothing could be done until they had a Drivers Licence with their current address. Oh, and their TARION new home warranty certificate too, to prove they owned the house. Grumbling, Shelina subjected herself to the tender mercies of the Motor Vehicle Bureau, to obtain a temporary licence showing her new address. Meanwhile, Doug visited their lawyer, who (for a fee) provided a copy of their TARION certificate.

"Y'know, I mailed the original certificate to you last week," said the lawyer.

"Yeah, and that's the problem: It's being held hostage at the post office by Attila the Hun's sister," replied Doug, grinding his teeth. The couple returned to the post office, where they were blessed with the same clerk.

"Here's my Drivers Licence showing our new address," said Shelina. The clerk examined it minutely, in case it was counterfeit, then sniffed. "And here's a copy of our TARION certificate," said Doug. The clerk sniffed again as she took the document, then suddenly beamed.

"We need the original certificate," she announced happily.

Feeling like they'd just fallen down Alice's rabbit hole, Doug gritted: "It's in that pile of our mail you're holding back there, that we can't get delivered until you give us the key for our mailbox!"

"Rules are rules," intoned the bureaucrat, looking past Doug to the next victim in line awaiting torment.

"Look, you have to understand that there's bills becoming overdue in that mail you're holding, and if we don't pay them, our hydro, gas and other services will be cut off!"

"Sir, I work for the government. I don't have to understand anything," said the clerk.

At this point, Doug left. It was self-preservation; he wished to forestall a heart attack. Shelina planted herself firmly in front of the clerk and, with a resolve of granite honed by years of dealing with obtuse bureaucracy, demanded she summon her manager. The clerk refused, being quite capable of abusing customers on her own. Shelina was implacable and the confrontation escalated to where another Canada Post employee, awakened from his nap by the shouting, unearthed the manager.

Eventually, the clerk dumped a pile of mail on the counter in front of Shelina. "Here's your mail," she growled, still defiant. "Now leave."

"Not. Yet." Shelina muttered, despite having been there an hour. She flipped through the mail and extracted a thick legal-sized package from their lawyer. Tearing it open, she removed the original TARION document.

"Here," she said, thrusting it at the clerk. "Now give me my damn mailbox key!"

I believe bureaucrats have quietly taken over the world.

The Skunk Whisperer

Most families have an eccentric uncle stashed someplace. Mine is called Matt and he lives near Ottawa, happily retired after decades at an obscure government job that he refuses to clearly describe.

You've heard of horse and dog whisperers; gifted folks who can talk soothingly to an animal, getting it to do what they want. Uncle Matt fancied himself a skunk whisperer.

It originated in his youth. Freshly-married, he and Carrie, his honey, were on a camping trip. Arriving at a sold-out campground, they pitched camp in a cramped "tent city" in the overflow lot.

As twilight deepened, they doused their Coleman lantern and snuggled into their sleeping bag. Looking out their tent's zipped-up screen door, they saw a captivating shadow show in the tent directly - and closely - opposite. Its occupants, another young couple, didn't realize that a lit lantern inside a nylon tent clearly outlines whatever goes on. The lady was kneeling and slowly disrobing next to the supine gentleman. Sleep was not in their immediate future.

Pillowing their heads on crossed arms, Matt and Carrie were enjoying the free show when right in front of them waddled the biggest skunk they had ever seen. The creature stopped and stared at them. Creature and campers were at eye level.

Terrified the skunk would let fly at close range through the flimsy screen, Matt started speaking, low and calm, asking it to please move on. The skunk cocked its head. Matt kept speaking in soothing tones.

Finally, the striped stinker lumbered away. My aunt and uncle were so relieved, they didn't mind that the shadow couple had extinguished their lantern.

Ever since, Matt's nickname had been The Skunk Whisperer. In countless retellings, the story became legendary.

The problem with legends is when the hero believes his/her own.

Many decades later, in the now-retired Matt's neighbourhood, garbage cans were being ransacked at night. A large black and white culprit was glimpsed. Well aware of his legend *(ad nauseam)*, neighbours prevailed upon Matt to murmur the skunk away.

Uncle Matt lay in wait, nursing a thermos of coffee. A werewolf moon painted the backyard in eerie paleness. The underbrush rustled. A shadow detached and plodded up to Matt's garbage can. Showtime!

Crouching, Matt sidled towards the skunk, speaking softly, soothingly. The critter's head whipped around. Beady eyes glared in the moonlight. Matt continued speaking, hunkering closer, encouraging Pepe Le Pew to please relocate his nocturnal foraging two streets over, where the homeowners had terrible taste in lawn ornaments.

He was now within touching distance. Right where the varmint wanted him. It turned, flipped up its tail, and expressed its candid opinion of mumbling fools interrupting its evening buffet. It emptied both of its anal musk sacks at once, blasting Matt with twin streams of its distinctive perfume.

Whispering forgotten, Matt bellowed loud enough to wake the neighbourhood as the noxious spray hit his face and chest. Temporarily blind, eyes watering, nose dripping, nauseated, he banged into the house, groped along the wall for the back door, then fumbled inside to the shower.

Standing in the spray for an eternity, cleansing water cascading over his upturned face, he couldn't understand why his vaunted Skunk Whispering power had failed. Aunt Carrie knew, had known for decades, but had kept it secret to preserve his fragile male ego. She finally told him as she double-bagged his clothes for the garbage:

The following morning at that campsite long ago, while Matt was off using the communal bathroom, Carrie had discovered that the huge skunk was actually the tame pet of a family two tents away.

Its scent glands had been removed.

Over the next several days, Matt endured much neighbourly ribbing about his abject failure to whisper away the skunk. He said it was due to seasonal allergies.

However, the foul freeloader still waddled through everyone's yard each night, poaching their canned garbage, causing much clutter and clatter. Something had to be done and Matt, anxious to repair his reputation, elected himself as the person to do it.

Not one to spend a dime unless his life depended on it, Matt refused to hire a professional exterminator. Besides, a pro would charge $200 and, complying with the law, only relocate the creature one kilometre from where it was caught. That was nuts; Pepe would be back noshing on their trash in no time.

He didn't want to kill the critter, being a humane sort (it was also against the law). So he bought a suitable trap. Once caught, he would relocate the beastie far away in some forest where it belonged. (He first considered driving to Toronto to release it at the home of his former boss, Fred, the living definition of "idiot jerk," but Carrie talked him out of it.)

The trap had thick, firm wire mesh on its sides and bottom. The top was solid galvanized steel, as were the flip-up doors at both ends. The doors had strong springs. Once the skunk entered to eat the bait in the middle of the trap, it would step on a small metal plate, which released both spring-loaded doors.

Before dusk, Matt placed the bait (carrots and celery, which he certainly would not miss) and set the trap.

As dawn broke, the trap doors clanged shut. Awakened, Matt and Carrie discovered they had an agitated unwilling guest. Matt donned his gardening grubbies and sallied forth to deal with Pepe.

Uncle Matt, now religiously cautious following his bilious baptism, had thoroughly researched skunk behavior. He'd learned that skunks don't spray what they can't see. So he carefully approached the trap from one of the solid metal ends, hidden from the varmint's view.

Reaching the cage without incident, he picked it up by its

sturdy top handle. He grunted with the effort; *Monsieur* Le Pew was large and heavy, about two feet long, bushy tail included, and a good 12 pounds. Holding the cage away from him, end-on, he carried it to his station wagon.

He forgot that the cage bottom was see-through wire mesh. As soon as Pepe espied the legs of the fool who had incarcerated him, he let fly. The pungent yellowish oily stream soaked Matt's jeans and he grimaced as the toxic smell burned into his nostrils.

He placed the cage, still end-on to him, in the rear of his car, which he had lined with a tarp beforehand. Good thing too; both cage and critter reeked.

He shut the lift gate, walked to the driver's seat, and stopped. No way was he going to sit on his nice leather seats in those odious jeans!

He looked at the house, at Carrie scowling behind the window of the closed (and locked) door. No way was she letting him inside to change. He hollered for her to at least throw him a fresh pair of jeans, in the name of humanity. She didn't move.

Matt got into his car and drove off. Behind him, in a heap on the driveway, lay his jeans.

He drove for about 30 km, then pulled into a small meadow bordered by dense forest. He parked near a massive oak that dominated the open field.

He carefully lifted the trap from the car. Walking to the other side of the oak tree, he placed it on the ground. En route, Pepe sprayed his legs again, but Matt had wrapped the tarp around him like a skirt for just this eventuality. However, the intense smell made his eyes water. He fought down nausea.

Pointing one end at the woods, standing behind the other end, he released the door. The skunk shot out like school kids at the 3:00 bell. Ignoring the beckoning forest, it twisted around and ran straight for the oak tree.

Matt swore. The skunk was now between him and his car!

Staying 15 feet away (the limit of its spray, according to his research), he edged towards the car. The skunk glared at him threateningly, and came out a few feet from the tree towards him.

Matt hastily backpedalled. Though skunks had poor vision, unable to clearly see objects over 10 feet away, they had excellent hearing and smell. And Matt sure did smell.

Matt retreated to the forest, then walked along the perimeter of the meadow until he reached the road on the other side of the car. Crouching, so the vehicle masked him from his tormentor, he ran to the station wagon and, abandoning his abhorrent skirt, flung himself inside through the passenger door.

Gunning the engine, he tore out of the meadow. He was halfway home before he realized he still wore rubber boots that had also been sprayed.

The intense *eau-de-skunk* made his head swim. He drifted from side-to-side in his lane. Five minutes later, a cop pulled him over.

The officer walked up. To confirm his suspicion that Matt was intoxicated, he stuck his head inside the window and breathed deep. Big mistake. The cop stepped back hastily, coughing like a three-pack-a-day smoker.

"Sweet Baby Jesus!" he gasped. "Skunk!"

Matt confirmed that yes, Sherlock, he'd been freshly sprayed and no, he was not going to step out of the car in his underwear.

Bent over, still coughing, the cop waved Matt on his way.

Arriving home, Aunt Carrie refused to let him in until he first scrubbed himself raw with copious amounts of soap, using the backyard garden hose. (He kept his undies on.) He was so miserable, he barely felt the ice-cold water.

He spent the next two days shampooing his car's interior, five times, especially the front seat, floor, and trunk. Ditto for the boots.

Three days later, their garbage cans were again raided by a skunk with a taste for trash.

Aunt Carrie insisted they call an exterminator. Uncle Miser ignored her.

Matt baited and set the trap. Next morning, he squinted at their prisoner from a safe distance. It was about the same size, but he couldn't tell if it was the one he'd already relocated, or a new looter who'd moved into the franchise's vacant territory.

Resolved not to repeat his previous mistakes, yet suspecting he would create all-new ones, he decided he needed reinforcements. He conscripted his son-in-law, Reg.

This time, Matt crept up to the trap with an old plastic tarp, again approaching from an end. Reaching the steel prison, he draped the tarp over it, then took off like fans after a rock star.

No reaction.

"Now for the tricky part," he said, as Reg gulped nervously. "The plastic's larger than the trap. See the extra material on the lawn? I'll tilt the trap to one side, while you quickly shove one end of the excess tarp underneath. Then we'll repeat the process with the other side. The trap will then be completely covered and we won't get sprayed."

Reg wondered, not for the first time, if other fathers-in-law were as hazardous to one's health.

The manoeuver went off without a hitch. (Knowing neighbours were watching, and knowing that a skunk in a dark enclosure just lay there quietly, Matt made a show of talking to his captive, hoping to recapture his Skunk Whisperer fame.) Using bungee cords to keep the plastic firmly wrapped around the trap, they carried it to the station wagon.

Just as they were about to place it inside, the skunk caught a glimpse of his captors through a small tear in the old plastic. He promptly let fly, dousing the inside of its cage. Though no fluid leaked out, the smell was intense. They drove to the meadow with all windows open.

This time, Matt was careful not to have the oak tree between them and the car. When they released the door, the black-and-white pillager exploded out and disappeared into the woods.

They returned home with the freshly-sprayed tarp and the skirt-tarp Matt had previously abandoned. Both tarps received multiple shampoos, as did the befouled car, again. Though neither Skunkbuster had been sprayed, they still reeked. Both wives insisted they take several showers before being considered compatible again.

Three days later, guess what? The neighbourhood trasheteria had another customer.

"If this is the same skunk, we should name it Boomerang," opined Matt.

"Let's spray-paint a bright orange dot on it. Then we'll know," suggested Reg.

"Great idea. *You* do it."

Reg dropped the subject.

Tired of shampooing his station wagon, Matt convinced Reg to use his van for prisoner transport, as it had a roof rack. They would lash the wrapped cage atop the van, so nothing noxious would get inside.

Bait. Set. *Clang!* Gotcha!

Cover. Tilt. Wrap. Exhale.

Both Skunkbusters left the trap, to rummage in the garage for the bungee cords. Princess Jessica, Matt's cute (and spoiled) eight-year-old granddaughter, walked over, concerned about the poor skunk's welfare. A Disney *Bambi* junkie, she believed Flower, Bambi's skunk buddy, accurately depicted his race.

She knelt and lifted a corner of the tarp, cooing at the critter.

Spray. Screams. Curses. Showers.

"Well, we still have that skunk to get rid of," muttered Matt, after the cacophony had died down somewhat.

"Yep," agreed Reg. "And I'm sure Jess didn't really mean it when she swore never to visit you ever, ever again. Dunno where she learned such salty language, though."

"Well, it wasn't from *my* daughter."

Bungee cords forgotten, they carried the cage to the car, holding the tarp tight around it. While tying the wrapped cage to the roof rack, a stiff breeze lifted an edge of the covering. Their captive hosed the roof.

Noses clogged, they drove to the now-familiar meadow and repatriated their prisoner back into woodland society.

Reg dropped Matt off at home, then drove to his own suburban domicile. He parked his van inside and closed the garage door. Ten minutes later, the van was back outside with Reg washing it furiously, thinking unkind thoughts about his father-in-law. The stench adorning the roof had infiltrated the house. Jessica, still traumatized, hurtled to the bathroom to hurl when the first whiff of skunk reached her.

Every window in the house was opened. Air freshener was liberally sprayed. Two cans worth.

Twilight. Three days later. A stinky scallywag again plundered the garbage. Uncle Matt groaned. Son-in-law Reg departed on a sudden business trip. Aunt Carrie, fed up, called the police.

Two officers arrived. Matt talked with one, outlining all he'd learned about trapping skunks. Meanwhile, unseen by Matt, her partner slipped into the backyard and blasted the skunk with a shotgun. *Buk-CHOOM!*

Matt, Carrie, and a host of gawking neighbours, were appalled.

"Why ... why did you *do* that?" demanded Matt. "There was no need!"

"Animal was rabid," gritted the officer. "I clearly saw foam at its mouth. Had to kill it, to protect everyone from rabies."

The cop came up to Matt, standing very close in clear violation of his personal space, and said: "You saw the foam too, Sir, if you'll just think back. Right?"

"Ah, right, right."

"Outstanding. Problem solved. Have a nice night."

The defrocked Whisperer consoled himself: *At least I didn't have to pay an exterminator.*

"In the land of the skunks,
he who has half a nose
is king."

– Chris Farley

Minefield of Meals

It's getting harder and harder to plan dinner parties these days. Whether you're hosting a soiree for 10 people, or 610, the challenge is the same: What *can* you serve? It's gone far beyond personal likes and dislikes.

Due to religious beliefs, some people won't eat pork or beef.

Because of food allergies, some diners must avoid shellfish, or peanuts, or tomatoes, or gluten, or dairy products, or sitting next to obnoxious relatives.

Medical reasons force other people to sidestep salt, or sugar, or deep-fried foods, or the bill at the end of the meal.

Some folks abhor fish (refusing to believe that our proto-ancestors crawled forth from the oceans millennia ago). Others shun fowl (having been thrashed once too often by feather pillows during pillow fights in their youth).

Then there are those who eschew any type of meat, preferring instead to pillage the plant kingdom. Others stoutly reject rabbit food, insisting on using the sharp incisors thoughtfully provided by evolution.

In my profession of association management, which includes organizing meals for hundreds of people attending annual conventions, choosing a menu that's acceptable to everyone has become a real nightmare. Even after you finally select items that should be universally acceptable, you still can't win.

For example: Despite a section on your convention Registration Form imploring delegates to note any dietary or religious meal restrictions, so that you may have ample time to arrange alternate foods, you are informed just as the banquet starts that you need four vegetarian, low-fat, low-sodium, lactose-free, nut-free, organic, kosher, lightly-watered, gently-picked-under-a-full-moon-by-Carmelite-nuns dinners.

As you enter the kitchen to tell the chef of this last-minute change, knowing that chefs feel the same way about last-minute changes as do bridezillas on their wedding day, you find yourself longing for an assistant to delegate this task to, because the chef has a very big, very sharp knife.

Nowadays, the hapless meal planner must navigate a minefield of dietary restrictions. It's enough to drive one mad - or to drive everybody to a smorgasbord. So, to help meal planners everywhere, I humbly offer this solution: serve dishes so unusual that they can't possibly be on anybody's can't-have list. How about this menu:

Choice of appetizer: Rattlesnake. Blue whale. Hippo. Served on toasted pita bread with jellyfish butter.

Choice of entree: Wombat. Fruit bat. Narwhal. Served grilled, basted with iguana sauce.

Choice of dessert: Earthworm. Madagascar Hissing Cockroach. Saskatchewan Cussing Bed Bug. Served with crunchy termite ice cream.

For special occasions: Duck-billed platypus. The ultimate unusual dish, since that critter doesn't know what to make of itself. It has fowl parts and beaver parts and swims underwater like a fish. It's a mammal that lays eggs. Because it's such a multiple-vehicle pile-up of various branches of the animal kingdom, it can't offend anybody. To appease the vegans, serve it atop a bed of organic greens.

Now, to wash it all down, you need a widely-acceptable beverage. Some folks can't have caffeine, so that eliminates regular coffee and tea. Others dodge decaf like the plague. Diabetics can't have sugar-infused pop, while many normal people can't stand artificially-sweetened pop. Some refuse to quaff tap water; others boycott bottled water. Lactose-intolerants can't guzzle milk; others are deathly allergic to soy-milk. I have a solution for that too:

Serve everyone single malt scotch. After a few shots, they'll swear they're drinking nectar of the gods (true).

The alternative is too ghastly to contemplate: Have everyone BYOB (Bring Your Own Banquet). What a classy dinner that would be. Hey, Tupperware could sponsor it.

I will eat anything that doesn't eat me first.

Eco-Baggage

These days, we're pressured to shop with reusable bags, instead of disposable plastic bags, to save the environment. Ordinary plastic bags clog landfills, blight landscapes, and take as long to decay as radioactive waste or Aunt Betsy's fruitcake.

However, I've noticed one major problem with this eco-trend: You end up with a plethora of eco-bags.

There's a specialized multi-chambered bag for the liquour store. Each grocery chain has their own monogrammed bag, as do hardware stores. Canadian Tire sells a green eco-bag (that is actually black). Costco sells them in big packages (naturally) of four bags (two regular-sized, two ginormous).

The harried consumer must now maintain an ever-growing stack of eco-sacks; far too many to carry while enviro-conscientiously walking or cycling. So we're forced to use our gas-guzzling vehicles to cart them around, which is not what the eco-warriors intended. (Car trunks should come equipped with a giant built-in file folder, alphabetized, to hold our many eco-bags. With smaller slots for each store's reward card.)

You have to be careful to use the right bag at the right store.

You can't visit the booze shoppe armed with a grocery eco-bag, because your bottles of wine and spirits will clang together alarmingly without the separate padded compartments of the special liquour bag. (LCBO employees no longer use plastic mesh protectors over the bottles, because plastic is the new evil. It's much more environmentally-conscious to risk smashed glass and spilled toxic liquid. In my view, the eco-safest place for these toxic liquids is inside humans, not seeping into our precious water tables.)

Similarly, you can't very well use the compartmentalized booze bags when grocery shopping (although the well-padded sections would keep veggies separate, eliminating the horror of bruised broccoli and crushed cauliflower, or the abomination of cross-pollinating asparagus and rutabagas). It would cause heated altercations, if not actual fisticuffs, if you walked into Sobey's with a Loblaw's eco-bag, or had the nerve to saunter into Home Depot carrying Canadian Tire's black bag.

And now there's concerns about bacteria build-up in reuseable bags. It's hazardous to one's health to be environmentally-conscious.

What about buying a generic, logo-free bag, to use everywhere? Well, it's not that simple.

Many generic eco-bags are made of hemp. That's another word for marijuana. So you could be accosted by undercover police as you shop, demanding proof that you have a medical disability permitting marijuana use. The worst case scenario: hordes of shoppers toking up on their hemp sacks in their cars, and then stumbling into the store buying up everything in the snack aisle. Which will deprive our teenagers of a major food group.

Other generic eco-bags are made of recycled plastic, the very substance we are now condemning. Irony of ironies, these enviro-totes are not recyclable at many depots after they've worn out.

Some stores are using paper bags again. I don't follow that logic. Isn't it better to have more trees alive and oxygenating, instead of less plastic in landfills?

And it's far more difficult to carry paper bags from car to house, than plastic bags with their handy handles. While I can carry about eight plastic bags in one trip, I can only safely manage two paper bags. (Important tip: Don't place them on wet ground while you fumble for your door keys. Trust me.)

This means four trips compared to the previous one, which wastes my precious energy resources. (Unless this is a conspiracy to make us exercise more, in which case it infringes on our democratic freedom of laziness.)

I assure gentle readers and zealous tree-huggers that this was written with tongue in cheek and eco-bag(s) in hand.

Bludgeoned by Bureaucracy

A reader of my funny stories related this true tale to me. I've changed some details to protect the afflicted.

This reader (let's call her Lucinda) has a sister (let's call her Tina) who lives in a Northern Manitoba village so remote that it's only accessible by air or, during Spring floods, by water.

One year, Tina decided to send Lucinda a Christmas present. To save on exorbitant shipping charges, she ordered a yellow (Lucinda's favorite colour) sweater from the catalogue of a national department store chain, for delivery to their Peterborough store, where Lucinda would simply waltz in and pick it up.

Both sisters had no inkling of what they had unleashed.

It started innocently enough: Early one week, Lucinda received a phone call from the Peterborough store that she had a package waiting for her. The following weekend, she drove to the store and presented herself at the pickup counter, identifying herself by name and address.

Not good enough. She was asked for her phone number. She gave it. The clerk could find no record of a package under that number. Lucinda said it was a present sent by her sister in Manitoba.

Well then, did she have her sister's phone number?

"What do you need that for?" said Lucinda, getting irritated. "She's in Manitoba! I don't have her number memorized. You obviously have my number somewhere, because someone here called to tell me the package is here!"

Irrelevant. She needed her sister's phone number to take possession of her gift.

Lucinda left, and did what any Canadian would do: Went to Tim Horton's for a coffee and donut to soothe her rattled nerves.

She returned home and was fetching her sister's number when the phone rang. It was Tina. She had just been called by the store and warned that they would only hold the package for two more days, so Lucinda better come and get it.

Lucinda related her attempt to do just that. Hanging up, she called the store and endured voice mail hell until she finally connected with a manager. She gave him an earful. He apologized and promised that upon her return, the gift would be ready.

She returned to the pickup counter the very next day. Blessed relief: She was not asked for any phone number.

She was asked for her store credit card.

"But I don't have a credit card for your store," Lucinda said.

Well then, did she have her sister's store credit card?

"Now how the hell would I have that?" exclaimed Lucinda, certain now she was in a level of Dante's Inferno. "She's in friggin' MANITOBA! And isn't it ILLEGAL to walk around with others' credit cards? Besides, this is a GIFT!"

Serene with the power of impenetrable bureaucracy, the clerk admonished her to calm down. Lucinda smiled tightly and said this was her second visit to claim her parcel, a manager yesterday assured her everything would be arranged, the store had just informed Tina that the gift was about to be returned, so there was NO WAY she was leaving WITHOUT HER CHRISTMAS PRESENT.

The clerk blinked. "Well then, do you have your husband's store credit card?"

Fortunately, Lucinda had a husband and luckily he had a credit card from that store. She didn't have it with her, of course. However, even more luckily, hubby was home when his frazzled wife called him on her cell.

The card number was provided. The package was grudgingly surrendered.

Unwrapping the package on Christmas Day, Lucinda discovered the store had shipped a maroon sweater, instead of a yellow one. In the wrong size.

She lacked the stamina to return it.

Thankfully, I never receive presents from my sister.

Dental Floss

On a routine visit, my dentist wondered why I hadn't written a funny story about such experiences. I replied:

"Becauf there'ff nuffink honey aboot gwyine to th' dentiff." Or something like that. Various instruments of oral amusement were occupying my mouth, traditionally the perfect time for dentists to ask questions.

Clearly understanding what I said (a supernatural ability bestowed upon dentists along with their degree), she related the following tale as proof that funny things do indeed occur at these Houses of Pleasure:

Early in her career, as she was establishing her practice, a young lad reluctantly plopped into her chair for his regular checkup. Chairs back then were covered in fabric instead of smooth vinyl. Her examination rooms were separated from the waiting room by partitions that ended several feet from the ceiling, so that air (and sound) circulated throughout the office.

As she lowered the chair from an upright to a reclining position, the small eight-year-old slid downward, so that his head ended up below the headrest. The dentist grabbed him under the armpits and hauled him upwards towards the headrest. This loud cry was heard by everyone in the waiting room:

"Stop! You're pulling down my pants!"

The boy was wearing corduroy trousers, that venerable staple of every lad's wardrobe back then, thanks to their mothers' corduroy fetish. The corduroy stuck to the fabric of the chair, so that pants stayed put while occupant moved up.

Horrified and red-faced, the dentist dashed into the waiting room, assuring everyone, especially the mother who had left her chair and was inbound to her son, that it was an accident and she was not some evil pervert.

Another reason why boys hate corduroys.

One fine day, whiling away the time enjoying my first (and hopefully last) root canal, I challenged myself to create a funny story about dentist visits. The above tale notwithstanding, I came up empty.

It's understandable: I've never met anyone with a kind thing to say about a trip to the tooth-mechanic, no matter how nice, competent and gentle they are. Tell a child or an adult that tomorrow is their dentist appointment, and both quail deep inside, desperately concocting excuses to postpone the visit. ("Can't go; my pet aardvark needs a flu shot.")

And, just like your car mechanic, you often end up with a surprising bill after your dentist checks under your hood.

Actually, it's a wonder dentists don't develop serious self-esteem issues, since every workday, most everyone they encounter doesn't like them very much. Oh sure, when it's over, many patients smile, say thanks and even shake hands, but all they really want is to get out of there pronto.

Adding insult to injury: We have an annual Doctor Appreciation Day in our fair city (which didn't stop my doctor from abandoning his practice and 2,000 patients to grab more money elsewhere), but there's no similar day for our faithful dentists.

Relaxing on her comfy chair, soothed by the delightful sound (like a jolly calliope) of the drill in my mouth, trying to ignore her muttered "oops," I felt sorry for these skilled, yet unappreciated, tooth jockeys.

My sympathetic feelings lasted until the long operation ended and I was presented with the bill.

Yow!

She didn't give me enough freezing to numb *that* pain.

Next time, it's a string attached to a doorknob and the diseased tooth. "The old ways work best," my Grampa always said. "Much cheaper, too."

Grampa died toothless.

Nine out of ten dentists claim that "people don't mind having root canals these days." (Yeah, right.)

Animal Crackers

Our son remarked one day that denizens of the animal kingdom have it easy. They don't suffer from half the afflictions that humans endure. (Although when they can't do their jobs anymore, they don't get fired or retired. They get eaten.)

Just imagine a cheetah with asthma: "Wait up! (pant, wheeze) Will you zebras *please* stop running so I can kill one of you?"

How about an ape with arthritis? "I'm not swinging through that jungle; my joints are *killing* me today. Have Tarzan call me a cab."

A shark with a sensitive stomach: "I don't care if we're supposed to be the scavengers of the seas. No way I'm eating *that*. It's been dead for *days*."

A near-sighted eagle: "Ah, from this high up, I *think* that's a rabbit. Or a cat. Lord, I hope it's not a skunk, like last week. The heck with it, I'll order pizza."

An circus elephant allergic to peanuts: "Some kid slipped me a peanut once and I went into anaphylactic shock. Fell over and crushed three clowns. And you should have *seen* the size of the Epipen needle they had to use on me!"

A diabetic bumblebee: "I can't make honey anymore, 'cause it sends my blood sugar sky-high. So my hive turfed me out, calling me a useless freeloader. Well, I'll show them! I'm no freeloader! I'll become a politician."

How about a cow who's tired of the vegan life? "If I eat another blade of grass, I'll go mad. I'm fed up with rabbit food. Give me a steak. Medium-rare. I don't care if I'm related to it."

A ferocious tiger with strep throat: "Meow."

An obese weasel: "Can't ... get ... through ... hole ... in ... henhouse ... wall. Ah, forget it! I'll split a pizza with that near-sighted eagle."

A black bear with male pattern baldness: "Next male hiker I

see with a full head of hair? He'd better be a fast runner, 'cause there's my toupee. I don't even care about the colour. In fact, blond, red, or even silver hair would give me a cool, punk look."

A beaver with rotten teeth: "I simply can't chew another stick. Too painful. That'll teach me not to floss regularly. I'm relocating next to a sawmill with a big pile of sawdust."

A woodpecker with chronic migraines: "I can't pound my beak into another tree. My head is just killing me. Well, I'm tired of a bug diet anyway. I'm switching to ratatouille."

A penguin who's afraid of the water: "I'm moving to Pittsburgh. My cousin Irving can get me a job with a hockey team there."

A cat who's lactose (and people) intolerant: "Get rid of that saucer of milk, or else I'll hack up a furball into your latte. Don't you have any white wine, or beer? Tequila?"

A claustrophobic ant: "I can't stand crowds anymore. And those long narrow tunnels drive me crazy! I gotta be out in the wide open spaces. I'll become a cowboy."

A mountain goat with a fear of heights: "*Why* did I climb so high and how the heck am I *ever* going to get down? How come only stranded human climbers get rescued? Oh great, now I'm getting a nose bleed. That's gonna leave a stain on my white fur."

A dolphin with clinical depression: "Sea World fired me. I was the only dolphin there who wasn't smiling. I just didn't feel like constantly cavorting for the crowds, y'know? All the jumping, the splashing, the happy chiruping, the waving with the fins. And for what? A bucket of fish scraps. Phooey!"

I know some dogs in my neighbourhood who need therapy.

The Time of the Hapless Mariner

Certain people are born to be mariners. Wind and wave are in their blood; the far horizon beckons like an eager used car salesperson; the ground is much too stable to be tolerable.

My brother is not one of those people.

The clues were there, even in his early years.

My brother (let's call him Jack) had an older sibling (let's call him me). In the 1960s, in my early teens, I learned to sail on Lake St. Louis, a vast aquatic playground west of Montreal whose polluted waters looked so inviting - until you fell into them. Siblings being what they are, Jack too had to become a sailor, no matter what it took.

What it took were a lot of tippings. Time and again he and his crew were pitched into the unsanitary drink as their sailboat tried to become a submarine. (It was during all those impromptu dunkings that Jack learned his colourful vocabulary; as his crew surfaced, sputtering, and voiced their candid opinion of his sailing skills.)

Yet he persevered - stubbornness is a family heirloom - and eventually got his sailing credentials. Then, of course, he had to prove himself a better sailor than his older brother.

This meant he took risks, such as sailing in winds much too strong for my liking. Utterly fearless, Jack revelled in defying gale-force winds in our beloved family sailboat.

Built in Lunenburg, Nova Scotia, where they built the iconic Bluenose (I and II), our 17-foot vessel was sleek and sturdy. Jack reasoned, given her hardy Maritime heritage, that she was tough enough to take whatever nature could dish out on our big inland lake.

And she did.

Until that ominous overcast day when, despite my entreaties to stay ashore, he challenged a wind blowing like a Force Five hurricane. With an extremely nervous girlfriend as his crew, Jack sailed off into the dark tempest in our valiant craft, which sliced and bucked through the furious whitecaps faster than she had ever travelled before. Exultant, my brother whooped at the speed.

The fact that he was the only sailboat out that day bothered him not a whit.

Then the howling squall snapped the windward stay holding up her mast, causing the mast to tear through her deck as it fell and blowing the boat, helpless and shattered, down the lake towards Montreal's infamous Lachine Rapids, a treacherous maelstrom that had devoured many a Voyageur canoe during the fur trade.

Minutes away from entering the deadly rapids, they were miraculously rescued by the marine police. Our once-proud sailboat, now looking like it had lost a war with King Neptune himself, was carted home and dumped on our front lawn, marooned out of her natural element, there to be gawked at by *tsk-tsking* neighbours.

I could hardly bear to look at her; every time I did, conflicting emotions flooded me: A profound sadness mingled with a powerful urge to throttle my unrepentant brother (who blamed the shipwreck on shoddy construction).

As soon as our sailboat was repaired, our father sold her.

"Now there'll be no more of that stupidity," Dad proclaimed, amputating a cherished part of my youth.

Years later, married and now a father himself, Jack moved his family to the prairies. His wife, Sally (formerly the terrified girlfriend during the hurricane cruise), sighed in relief: There could be no more aquatic misadventures in this dry land of grain, bison and perogies.

She soon learned that there are indeed lakes on the prairies; you just have to find them, because jealous westerners conceal their whereabouts from outsiders.

Jack settled in Edmonton. Heeding the mariner's siren song in his blood, he eventually found a lake suitable for boating, albeit an hour's drive from Alberta's capital.

Then, to Sally's horror, he bought a sailboat and started sailing again. In gustier and gustier winds.

Finally, after countless tippings and other mishaps, he had to drydock his sailing hobby. Seems he could no longer get a crew to ship out with him. His family and friends refused to leave the safety of *terra firma*.

Since the British Navy's practice of having brutal Press Gangs kidnap men to crew its ships was unfortunately no longer allowed, Jack admitted defeat and grudgingly sold his sailboat.

He used the proceeds for a down payment on a new motor boat. A significant portion of her 20-foot length housed an engine powerful enough to challenge the water speed record in the Guinness Book.

Jack swore on a stack of life jackets that he would be a prudent captain. He promised to cruise at sensible speeds, resisting the urge to slam down the throttle and rocket across the lake like a demented banshee.

His family believed him and booked passage aboard his mighty vessel.

They should have known better.

After a harrowing summer of high speeds, tight turns, near misses and constant spray crashing over the gunwales, accompanied by frequent screams, Jack's wife and two daughters swore off boating for good. From then on, the only time they would get near a body of water was when they took a bath.

My brother was shocked and disappointed. He couldn't understand why, considering he had so thoroughly enjoyed himself that summer.

However, he still had an eight-year-old son: Charlie.

As a trade-off for risking his life to go boating with his dad, Charlie insisted Jack teach him how to fish. Jack reluctantly agreed; on the one hand, it was an opportunity to bond over a classic father-son pastime, which would surely lead to albums of fond memories in later years.

On the other hand, besides being a daredevil mariner, Jack had another peccadillo: He was extremely fastidious about the cleanliness of his new boat. Chrome and fibreglass sparkled; carpet and upholstery were immaculate. Anyone bringing the slightest morsel of dirt or sand aboard was keelhauled.

Since fishing was known to be a somewhat grubby sport (bait, fish slime, weeds, dirt, blood, spilled beer, tears), Jack took steps to minimize any possibility of befouling his lovely vessel.

From a friend who used to go deep-sea fishing off Florida, Jack acquired a huge Red Devil lure, obviously made to attract Moby Dick. He figured no Alberta fish would ever bite that, so Charlie could fish all he liked and the chances of actually catching anything were as slim as his daughters staying virgins until they married.

In the unlikely event something did mouth the gargantuan lure, Jack brought a large plastic storage container. He would place the finny catch inside, thus preserving the cleanliness of his boat.

Both clad in shorts and t-shirts, father and son loaded up their craft and cast off.

From the parking lot of the marina, a hundred yards from the water's edge, mother and daughters waved until the boat was out of sight (which didn't take long at the speed Jack was travelling), then high-fived themselves that they remained safe ashore.

It was mid-afternoon when Jack throttled back from hyperspeed and anchored at a likely spot near some weeds. Charlie unclenched his white-knuckled grip on the seat and watched as his dad assembled the fishing rod.

Jack brought his son up to the bow and instructed him on the proper casting technique. Then he attached the whale lure and left him to it.

My brother sauntered sternward, kicking off his sandals and snagging a beer from the cooler en route, looking forward to a relaxing afternoon dozing in the comfy lounge seat while Charlie fished fruitlessly.

On his very first cast, the boy hooked something so powerful that it almost jerked the rod out of his young hands. He hollered for his dad to come help.

Jack charged up to the bow and grabbed the rod as the line started zinging out like it would never stop. He realized just how big the fish was when he tried to reel it in. He managed a few turns of the reel, then the unseen beast took off and the line sang out once more.

An epic battle between man and dinner started, which took quite some time. Jack felt like the title character in Hemingway's *The Old Man and the Sea*.

Finally, exhausted, the fish allowed Jack to bring it in next to the boat. Equally exhausted, Jack peered down into the muddy water for a glimpse of the Leviathan they'd caught. What he saw caused his spirits to soar. Then sink.

It was huge. And it was a Slough Shark.

Elsewhere in Canada, the fish was known as the Northern Pike. But Albertans called it a "Slough Shark", because of the shallow lakes in which it lived, its fighting ferocity, and its slimy skin. (The lakes in Northern Alberta are shallow; being called mud puddles or sloughs by the locals.)

Jack quailed. No way he wanted that greasy creature aboard his spotless vessel.

Then he looked at Charlie, who was regarding the behemoth with eyes as big as those of an administrator of a non-profit organization lusting after a government grant. He couldn't disappoint his boy.

Now catching a monster pike and actually landing it into one's boat were two very different things, as Jack soon discovered. The rod bent alarmingly when he tried to lift the fish out. And he almost lost his grip as the fish thrashed violently when it realized it was leaving its favorite habitat.

Afraid he'd lose his hard-won catch, Jack yelled for Charlie to fetch the net.

Jack entrusted the rod to his son's eager grip. He submerged the net and got it under the pike, then with great effort, heaved it out of the water and into the large plastic container.

The fish barely fit. In awe, Jack said:

"It's easily three, maybe three and a half, feet long, if it's an inch! And it's gotta weigh at least 30 pounds!"

Father and son hugged each other in triumph.

Then they discovered the other reason locals nick-named the

pike a Slough Shark. It smelled awful.

Holding their noses, they both stared at their prize.

Its lean green and white spotted body seemed to be all muscle. Its angular mouth, filled with large needle-sharp canine teeth, gnashed repeatedly. Baleful eyes glared up at its captors.

"We're really gonna enjoy eating you, buddy," said Jack, paying a fisherman's ultimate compliment.

Unimpressed, the smelly, mucus-covered pike writhed in its plastic prison and gnashed some more.

The writhing and gnashing went on for some time. When it stopped, Jack wrapped his hand in a towel, so he wouldn't have to touch the slimy skin, and gripped the fish while he used pliers to gingerly remove the lure from the underslung duckbill jaw. He had heard what those wicked teeth did to unwary fishermen's fingers. However, the fish lay immobile during the entire operation. Jack concluded it was dead.

Whistling, Jack picked up the container and carried it towards the stern.

Half-way there, the beast jerked into sudden life and flipped itself right out of the container!

It landed on Jack's pristine carpet and flopped all over the floor, leaving stinky slime in its wake.

Aghast at the odorous mess it was causing, Jack lunged for the fish. But those nasty snapping teeth forced him to back off. Cursing, he wondered how long it would take the thing to die and if his carpet would ever be clean again.

At last, it lay still. Pleased that it finally had the decency to expire, my brother retrieved the towel and went to replace the creature in the container.

As he approached, the pike started thrashing violently again. Jack recoiled with a surprised yelp.

Angry at how long the damn fish was taking to leave this mortal coil, Jack resolved to help it on its way by humanely putting it out of its misery.

He grabbed a paddle and whacked the pike a good one on its head. Then twice more, to be sure. One can't be too humane.

Satisfied the fish's spirit had finally gone to that Great Lake In The Sky, and salivating at the thought of its sweet white flesh in that Big Buttered Skillet In The Kitchen, Jack flung down the paddle and reached for the body.

The allegedly-dead pike suddenly twisted around with an energy it hadn't displayed since its capture. Its keen teeth snapped mere millimeters from my brother's ankle.

Letting out a (censored) cry of alarm, Jack leapt away from that terrible mouth. He then discovered that leaping is not a wise thing to do when one's carpet is covered with fish slime.

Flailing his arms, Jack skidded into the side of his boat, smashing a little toe hard into unyielding fibreglass. The toe broke instantly. He howled in pain. Behind him, the still-thrashing Slough Shark looked like it was smiling.

Enraged, Jack grabbed the paddle again and laid into the demon from the depths with gusto. *Mucho* gusto.

Cries of: "Die, damn you! DIE!" filled the air, scaring nearby birds into wing. His young son squealed and retreated to the bow, as far away from his demented dad as he could get.

When Jack was finally done, the creature resembled something that might have been attacked with a meat tenderizer. It now only vaguely looked pike-like.

Just to make absolutely sure of its demise, Jack grabbed a screwdriver from his toolkit and rammed it through one of the beast's eyes into its brain.

"There, now you're well and truly dead, damn you," snarled Ahab of Alberta.

The pike's dark-spotted tail twitched. Jack stared, unbelieving. The body arched and the tail smacked hard on the carpet. The jaws clacked together.

Uttering a cry of rage, Jack dove for his fishing tackle box and unearthed a large Bowie knife, which he then used to saw the fish's head clean off.

Satisfied it was irrefutably dead, he flung both head and body into the container and cracked open a much-needed beer (for medicinal purposes, to numb the agony of his broken toe).

It was only then that he noticed his son.

Charlie cowered in the bow, sitting with his knees pulled up to his chin, regarding his father with horrified tear-filled eyes. What should have been a time-honored father-son bonding adventure in the Great Outdoors, had turned into a traumatic orgy of death and destruction.

They motored home in silence.

After a visit to the hospital, it took Broken Toed Jack the entire weekend to clean the boat, especially to get the repugnant smell out of the carpet.

From that day forward, Charlie refused to eat fish.

He also swore off boating with Dad.

Despondent, crewless, Jack finally realized that he was not meant for the life of a mariner. Just like politics and honesty, he and water simply did not mix.

With heavy heart, he sold his prized vessel to his next-door neighbour.

The following weekend, Jack watched in astonishment as his son cheerfully departed with his next-door buddy and his dad to have fun in their family's new boat.

> *"He went like one that hath been stunned,*
> *And is of sense forlorn:*
> *A sadder and a wiser man,*
> *He rose the morrow morn."*

> – Samuel Taylor Coleridge,
> "The Rime of the Ancient Mariner"

"Dad, Don't Touch that Button!"

Every year, there's a special day for working parents: Take Your Kids to Work Day. That's when your little cherubs discover that their bossy mum and/or pop have bosses too. Your cherubs always return home with smug looks on their faces.

However, after years of careful observation, I've deduced that kids eventually grow up.

So I think we need another special day; this time for working children: Take Your Parents to Work Day.

Why not? Just like your kids saw you in a new light years ago, so too should you now observe them in their new careers. In fact, you deserve it. After all those years of helping them get through school, all the sacrifices and second mortgages, which finally paid off when they graduated and landed full-time jobs, don't you want to see them in action? To gloat?

It could be eye-opening.

Imagine your daughter the veterinarian, skillfully performing emergency surgery on a Labrador, or helping a cow through a difficult birth, while you stand watching all the blood and organs, the smell enveloping you, and thinking, as the floor comes suddenly up to meet you, that she used to be a little girl who fainted at the sight of blood.

Envision sitting next to your son the stockbroker, as he barks sell and buy orders over the phone, moves hundreds of thousands of dollars with a few rapid keystrokes on his computer, and you remember this was a kid who could never find his chequebook, much less balance it.

You watch in astonishment as your police officer offspring, who grew up so mild-mannered that she couldn't swat a fly, subdues an unruly brute twice her weight. While using some choice language that surely she never learned from you.

Fond memories of Sundays cooking with your son vanish as

you see him marshal a legion of assistants in a large hotel kitchen, feverishly preparing a banquet for 400 guests, in a cacophony of clanging pot lids, sizzling grills, steam, shouts, and the occasional flame. With you getting your hand slapped away from the chocolate-covered dessert confection that you were just going to taste a little of, honest.

My wife and I accompanied our son the TV Technical Director to the Toronto headquarters of Canada's largest national network. While watching, I perched on the corner of a console, where my firm, sculpted left buttock pressed a button that knocked the entire network off the air, coast-to-coast. A Big Boss stormed into the room, promising instant bloody death to the klutzy JAFO (Just Another ... Family ... Observer) responsible.

I said my son did it.

Of course, for such a day to work, parents would have to promise *just* to observe, curtailing their natural instinct to dispense advice, whether it's wanted or not. Otherwise, things could get rather embarrassing, like when your daughter is showing a couple through a gorgeous house, and they're dithering over whether to make an offer, and you blurt out that the house is absolutely *perfect* for them, even if it has a leaky roof and nowhere near enough storage space.

With some jobs, parental blathering would be dangerously distracting. Like when your son the air traffic controller is juggling 200 planes, or your daughter the lion tamer is surrounded by five slavering beasts.

Hmmm, maybe that's why there isn't a Take Your Parents to Work Day. Kids have enough challenges at work as it is, without heaping helpings of undesired parental advice on top of it.

Besides, isn't that what family holiday gatherings are for?

I am forever banned from TV stations.

Too Young to be Old

Completely unbeknownst to me, a significant milestone slipped by at our house recently:

My wife signed herself up with CARP.

CARP describes itself as "Canada's Association for the 50-Plus." It's a non-profit organization with the mandate to "preserve and protect 50-plus rights," in return for your 50-plus membership dollar.

I discovered this when a thick CARP member package arrived in our mailbox, addressed to my wife. She opened it and left it on the coffee table. Surprised to see it, I went through the materials, looking for ammunition with which to needle her mercilessly.

I learned that she hadn't just signed herself up.

There was a second membership card. With my name on it.

I was shocked. Not just that she had joined, but that she had conscripted me too, without my knowledge or consent. Why?

"Well, we're both over 50 and CARP offers many bargains to the 50-plus crowd, like insurance and travel discounts," she said. "Government has abolished mandatory retirement at 65, yet at the other end, retailers have lowered the age when you're eligible for seniors' discounts. So I figured it was time for us to take advantage."

While that may sound like prudent thinking, she fails to realize what else she's done.

Joining CARP means it's now official:

We're old.

I certainly don't consider myself old. There's lots more people far older - over 60 even - to enable me to maintain the illusion of still being "young."

Of course, in the eyes of my twentysomething son's generation, my wife and I should be making arrangements for a cemetery plot. He came home from work recently, bellyaching about some "old guy" there who thought he knew everything. Turned out the "old guy" was in his 30s.

Ouch.

Anyway, back to CARP. They have 400,000 members (now 400,002), and they've done a great job of concealing their true nature. Nowhere in their advertising or Member Directory do they admit what their acronym really stands for: Canadian Association of Retired Persons.

So there's two things wrong with us now being card-carrying CARPers: We both still work for a living and we're not *that* old.

That's why I had no intention of joining CARP until I was much, much older, like, say, 80. Or even 90. You know: undeniably *old*. (However, I recall I felt that way about fiftysomethings when I was a young buck of 16. So when I reach 80, I'll likely consider old people to be the 100-plus crowd.)

Regardless, right now, I have no interest in some of CARP's benefits, like Estate Planning, CPP Benefit Audit, Personal Emergency Response Service, special prices on hearing aid batteries, or a "Pimp My Ride" service for wheelchairs (Laz-Z-Boy recliner seat, beer cooler, Sirius satellite radio with deep-throb subwoofers, and a "sports package": racing stripes, off-road tires, turbo-charger, and five-point seat belt racing harness).

And I emphatically snub their Funeral Planning & Concierge Service. I know what a hotel concierge does: obtaining primo theatre and sports tickets, making dinner reservations, getting flowers, etc. What does a funeral concierge do for you after you're dead? Get you to the front of the queue at the Pearly Gates? Or, if you're headed the other way, negotiate an air-conditioned cell with Beelzebub?

I have no intention of "going gently into that good night." Going kicking and screaming is my plan.

I want CARP to give me a bumper sticker that reads: "I'm a CARP member, but I'm NOT old!"

Now officially elderly, I await the Grim Reaper. With a baseball bat.

The Scenic Route to Hell

Last winter, a good friend and his wife, eager to escape the cold and snow in Canada, flew to Arizona.

Landing in sunny, hot Phoenix, Doug and Shelina (pseudonyms, and you'll soon see why) changed into summer clothing and sandals, rented a convertible, powered down the top, and motored off into the mountains towards Sedona on the other side.

They had brought a portable GPS (Global Positioning Satellite) unit, which they programmed to guide them to Sedona via the scenic route. The device obediently did so, directing them in a sexless, annoying electronic voice.

Up and up they went. They had the whole road to themselves, in both directions, it being the off season. *(First red flag.)*

The air got steadily colder. Every roadside convenience store and gas station they passed was boarded up. *(Second red flag.)*

They passed a sign proclaiming they had just entered a state park and were at 7,500 feet in altitude. The air was quite cold now and they hadn't seen the sun for over an hour. Up went the rag top and on went the car heater. The gas gauge was edging past the half-way mark. *(Third red flag.)*

It started snowing. Doug joked: "Didn't we just leave this behind in Canada?"

The snow turned into a blizzard. "Apparently not," muttered Shelina.

As the road became slippery with snow, they realized their convertible had summer tires. *(Fourth red flag.)*

They passed a sign stating the ranger station was one mile away. "We'll stop there and ask how bad conditions are ahead," said Doug.

They came upon the station. Boarded up. *(There were now enough red flags waving to start the herd of bulls in Pamplona running.)*

Doug took a mental inventory of their supplies. Food: one apple and one banana. Warmth: one thin blanket. Emergency equipment if stuck in snow: back in his SUV in Canada. Cell phone to call for help: no signal this high in the mountains. Places they could go for help: all boarded up. Washrooms to answer a becoming-desperate need: ditto. Bushes to answer a becoming-desperate need: shrouded in snow.

They reprogrammed the GPS to cancel the scenic route and get them to Sedona via the most direct way.

"Recalculating," said the unit's irritating voice.

They came to a crossroads. The GPS instructed them to turn right. "I don't think so," said Doug. "That way seems to take us deeper into these mountains."

"Recalculating," said the obnoxious voice. It then ordered them to turn left, in the exact opposite direction!

Off they drove as the snowstorm howled around them. Reaching a T-junction in the road, the GPS said to take the turn, but Doug, now following his gut instinct, kept going straight.

"Recalculating," grated the high-tech pathfinder, which then agreed that the direction Doug had taken was correct.

Shelina concluded that: 1. Their GPS had the accuracy of an economist's predictions and 2. They were lost. (Back home, a tech person proclaimed that heavy snow affects satellite transmissions to GPS units. In such instances, employing an antique device known as a road map is more reliable.)

Eventually, thanks to Doug's gut and the occasional road sign, they emerged from the other side of the mountains, where the blizzard turned to rain, and found an open gas station. The car was running on fumes by then. Their bladders were about to burst.

They left the station without their GPS device. The last thing Doug heard as he turned away from the garbage can where he had angrily deposited it, was an aggravating voice echoing mournfully from the depths:

"Recalculating."

I don't need a GPS; my wife always tells me where to go.

The League of Pathetic Superheroes

Superheroes always have such magnificent powers: flight, invulnerability, super-strength, speed, eye beams, invisibility, looking great in tight spandex, and so on. However, the law of averages being what it is, if cosmic chance gave these heroes their neat powers, it stands to reason that some other folks received not-so-neat abilities.

Imagine a League of Pathetic Superheroes. Such as:

The Foghorn: Whenever he opens his mouth, a deep loud blare emerges. So he's never invited to any cool parties. Obvious secret identity: lighthouse keeper.

Yankee Clipper: Mild-mannered Boston hairstylist Clark Leityer by day, in costume he must give everyone he meets, male or female, a military-style crewcut, whether they want one or not. Nick-named "Buzz Lightyear."

Mr. Muffler: Used to be called The Human Exhaust due to his constant sickening flatulence. However, thanks to lobbying from environmentalists, he was fitted with an odour-scrubbing muffling device (it was either that, or spend a fortune buying methane credits). Has a kid sidekick named Speedy.

The Quizzer: Knows the correct answers to any quiz. Multi-millionaire thanks to her winnings on *Jeopardy*. Her brother is The Whizzer (you can figure out his power).

Captain Canada: A very different hero from the aggressive Captain America south of the border. Very conservative, our Captain considers himself in the minority. Constantly unsure of whether he has the backing of the people, he's afraid his power will be taken away at any moment. (His hidden lair is on Parliament Hill. Guess his secret identity.)

The Moisturizer: Her alter ego is a salesperson at a cosmetics counter (where she was bitten by a radioactive ant that had fallen into a jar of cold cream). Her power is to moisturize whomever she touches, leaving a slimy yet fragrant coating on their skin, which is amazingly effective in repairing dryness, age lines and blemishes. Then handing them a bill along with a free gift bag.

Speed Bump: A mutant gene constrains him to keep his Crimebustin' Cruiser precisely at the posted speed limit. Plus, he refuses to use the right-hand "slow" lane. Drives other motorists crazy. Panics if there's no speed limit sign on a long stretch of highway. Frequently travels with:

Mighty Map: Instantly knows where everything is when travelling in unfamiliar territory; he has an infallible GPS unit in his head. His weakness is he cannot orient himself, because he never knows where north is. He and Speed Bump often go on road trips with:

Capitaine Cuisine: A French-Canadian hero with the uncanny ability of knowing the best recipe for cooking anything. Comes in handy when their vehicle harvests some roadkill. His weakness: He flips out if he cannot obtain fresh seasoning for his recipes. And the right wine.

Stitchin Time: Compelled to sew up ripped clothing. Lurks around high schools, where she's busy for hours, despite angry student protests that their torn jeans are meant to be that way. She's convinced the kids are being mind-controlled by her evil nemesis: Jake the Ripper. In love with:

Laundromatt: Matt T. Sunlight in civilian life, he is driven to do laundry (the T stands for Tide). Obsessed with the neverending battle against dirt, he frequents football, soccer and rugby games, where he strips players of their soiled clothing for immediate laundering in his Washmobile (festooned with Maytag logos, his sponsor). He has the largest fan club of any superhero, composed entirely of women.

My own pathetic superpower? Blinding villains with the glare off my bald head. When evil threatens, summon the colossal **Chrome Dome!** (Sunny days only.)

I defend truth, justice, and the Canadian way (forced bilingualism, excessive taxation, and hockey).

The Things You Do for Love

Lynda screamed at her neighbour: "No! Stand down, Cletus! It's not for dinner! It's a pet!"

But I'm getting ahead of myself ...

One of our nieces in Edmonton found a nice guy with whom she wouldn't mind spending the rest of her life. Happily, he felt likewise. So they moved in together and declared couplehood. (They eventually got married, in a charming outdoor ceremony involving cupcakes and a llama, but that's another story.)

One day, their union produced something small, squirmy and slobbery, that needed almost-constant attention and was nowhere-near toilet-trained: a puppy.

Our niece (let's call her Lynda) joyfully bear-hugged her beau (let's call him Mark), who had presented her with this unexpected gift, rescued from the local SPCA. Meanwhile, said gift celebrated its release from incarceration by christening their new don't-pay-a-cent-for-18-months couch.

Lynda named the extremely-energetic male dog, jet black in colour with considerable Labrador in him, "Ferro." (Mark discovered months later that Ferro was the last name of her high school crush. After that, Lynda found herself taking the mutt for most of his walks.)

Lynda's best girlfriend, Cassie, was also owned by a pet. However, it wasn't a puppy. Being someone who always marched to her own drummer, Cassie had a miniature pot-bellied piglet. She called it "Cash," a take-off of her own name. (Considering the amount of carpeting Cash ruined as Cassie vainly tried to toilet-train him, the porker's name was apropos.)

Cassie noted how Lynda squealed with delight when she first saw Cash. Cash squealed right back. Cassie also observed how loving and attentive Lynda was with her own four-legged darling.

So it should have come as no surprise that, when Cassie and her husband scraped together enough real cash for a week's sojourn in Mexico, Lynda found herself shanghaied into minding the porcine Cash. Remembering how adorably cute the little piglet had been when last she saw it, Lynda readily agreed.

When she opened her door to greet her new house guest, Lynda was confronted with a two-foot-long, one-foot-high, fat 40-pound porker. Astonished, she looked at her friend.

Cassie shrugged and said: "He grew. Fast." Cash snorted and tried to nibble Lynda's bunny slippers.

Mark was less than impressed with their new boarder, but, for Lynda's sake, tolerated it. Ferro was ecstatic; the hyperactive pooch now had something new to chase around the house.

Lynda and Mark soon discovered that Cassie had been unsuccessful in getting Cash toilet-trained. After several unwanted gifts deposited around the house, including one in Mark's prized leather loafers, Cash found himself banished to the guest room. Which soon became a pigsty. Literally.

Besides a callous disregard for personal hygiene, the big pig had quite a temper. It strongly resisted doing anything it didn't want to do. As the young couple discovered the first time they tried to take it for a walk.

Both arriving home from work, the plan was for Mark to walk Cash while Lynda mucked out the hog's wallow previously known as their guest room. In the kitchen, as Mark attempted to fit the leash collar around the pig's fat neck, pandemonium ensued. Cash pulled away and let fly with high-pitched squeals of protest, louder than a car alarm. Mark hollered for Lynda's assistance. It took the two of them struggling with the uncooperative squalling porker to finally get his collar fastened.

"There," panted Mark, although neither he nor Lynda could hear a thing, being temporarily deafened by Cash's high-decibel cries. "Now I can take him out for a walk." He snapped a leash to the collar and opened the back door.

He pulled on the leash, but all four pig's feet dug in as Cash refused to budge. Mark pulled harder. Cash started squalling again, lowered his head and moved backward, dragging Mark forward.

Neither Mark nor Lynda noticed the pig's neck was bigger than its head.

The collar abruptly slipped off Cash's neck and zoomed past the smaller head. The pig was suddenly free. Mark's butt, followed by the rest of him, crashed to the floor.

With a high-pitched squeal of pure triumph, Cash took full advantage of his newfound freedom, barrelling past a stunned Mark and dashing straight out the door.

"Omigod!" yelped Mark. He scrambled to his feet and gave chase.

Ferro chose this moment to galumph into the kitchen, just in time to see Mark charge out the open back door. Always eager to chase something, anything, at any time, the young dog barked happily and bolted after Mark.

With a cry of alarm, Lynda grabbed for Ferro as he shot past her. She missed. So she too took off out the door.

It was winter in Edmonton. The streets and sidewalks in their suburban neighbourhood were sheathed in ice and hard-packed snow. Which didn't slow Cash down one little bit.

Thanks to his sharp hooves, the pig was extremely sure-footed. It was also extremely fast. It pelted down the centre of their street like a phrase rarely heard since the era of Brylcreem and fast cars with big tail fins: *greased lightning*.

It was around 6:00 p.m., and the neighbours enjoyed quite an unusual show: A large pot-bellied pig racing down the street, squealing mightily; chased by Mark, dressed for his planned walk and shouting ineffectually for the damn beast to stop; pursued by a two-month-old black thunderbolt yapping hysterically; trailed by Lynda bringing up the rear, her long red hair streaming out behind her and resplendent in her pink bunny slippers (not having been dressed for an outdoor jaunt). To add to the onlookers' amusement, Lynda slipped and slid as she tried to keep up.

The night air was filled with a colourful symphony of squeals, shouts, barks, and curses.

"Y'know, I'd pay to see a chase like this in a movie," laughed one neighbour, sipping his pre-dinner cocktail.

"I wanna film this to send to *America's Funniest Home Videos!*" said another neighbour, running to the hall closet for his camcorder. "I hope they won't mind doing it again for the camera."

A third neighbour spewed out a mouthful of home-brew. "My Gawd! Luanne! Fetch my rifle! I see dinner runnin' down th' street! We'll feast on ham hocks an' pork ribs tonight!"

"Bah! Young hoodlums!" groused a fourth neighbour. "What's a farm animal doing here in the suburbs anyway? It's that damn rock 'n' roll music that's the cause of all this!"

Two streets over, both pig and pursuer ran out of energy, so Mark was able to grab Cash. Ferro skidded to a stop to woof encouragement, allowing Lynda to catch up and nab him. Mark manhandled the squirming, squealing 40-pound porker homeward, while Lynda womanhandled the equally-squirming, barking 15-pound mutt.

En route to bringing home the bacon, Mark suggested several new names for the pig, like: "Pork Chops," or "Ham," or "Dinner."

Lynda remarked that a pig was the featured entree at Hawaiian luaus, after baking for hours in an in-ground lava rock oven.

"Sounds great. I'll borrow a shovel tomorrow," muttered Mark.

Turning a corner, they were almost bowled over by a running man carrying a rifle. The man quickly backpedalled and swung the gun up to his shoulder, cocking it as it went.

Lynda screamed at her neighbour: "No! Stand down, Cletus! It's not for dinner! It's a pet!"

The man slowly lowered his weapon. "Aw, buffalo chips! Well, looks like it's prairie dawg fer supper agin tonight. Dang!"

At home, with both animals securely behind closed doors again, the couple collapsed on the couch, exhausted.

"Maybe we should switch to goldfish instead," groaned Lynda.

When Cassie returned from her Mexican vacation, she was

surprised to find Lynda waiting on her doorstep.

"Your pig. In the car. Take him. Now." she gritted. "You can call me tomorrow an' tell me all about your trip. I gotta get home an' hose out our guest room."

Though Mark had been a good sport about the whole pig-sitting imposition, Lynda still felt she ought to do something special to make it up to him. So, one week later, she took a day off work to bake him his favorite dessert: homemade strawberry-rhubarb pie.

She had never baked a pie before in her life. But when you're in love, such things are of little consequence.

An Internet search unearthed what was assuredly a time-tested, grandma-approved recipe. Lynda printed it out, then went to the grocery store. Following the ingredients list, she sought out all the fixings needed to manufacture the mouth-watering confection, some of which were a challenge to find, it being the dead of winter.

Returning home, she propped up the recipe on the kitchen counter and carefully followed the instructions to create Guaranteed Awesome Strawberry-Rhubarb Pie.

She soon discovered one of the Laws of Cooking: "Volume of mess exceeds size of dish being created by a factor of four." In layperson's terms: her kitchen soon resembled a war zone. It was so bad, even the dog refused to enter, electing to stay in the doorway, whining, eyes wide with fear.

She spent hours preparing and cooking the strawberries and rhubarb. Everything would be authentically homemade. Well, except for the pie shell. She had cheated a little and bought a pre-made one. But she did craft the pie crust to cover the top, and it only took four tries to get it to roll out just right.

When it came time to assemble the pie, she realized in horror that she did not own a proper pie plate. A quick glance at the kitchen clock told her there wasn't enough time to dash to the store to buy one. So she used the thin aluminum foil plate that the pre-made pie shell had come in.

The assembled pie was big, heavy, and very thick. A monster

dessert, bulging under the crust that strained to cover it. Holding it under the plate, Lynda gingerly placed the pie in the hot oven, smiled in triumph, then retired to the livingroom for her first sit-down in many hours.

She had timed it perfectly. Mark arrived home from work to a house suffused with the rich aroma of baking pie. Surprised, he breathed deep of the familiar scent; something he hadn't smelled since Thanksgiving two years ago at his recently-divorced Mama's, just before Mama sold all her worldly possessions and decamped for a Tibetan pilgrimage.

"Good God, is that strawberry-rhubarb pie I smell?" he asked.

"Yeppir!" Lynda replied, beaming. "And I baked it myself from scratch! It's my way of saying thanks for putting up with my friend's damn pig."

Hugging and kissing ensued.

The oven timer dinged, causing *smoochus interruptus*. Donning thick oven mitts, Lynda opened the oven door and marvelled at the sight of her perfectly-cooked pie. It smelled wonderful.

Holding the steaming pie around the edges of the pie plate, she lifted it out of the oven and turned with a flourish, facing Mark.

"Ta da!" she said. Mark plopped himself down at the kitchen table and drooled expectantly, looking exactly like Ferro when his puppy chow was being prepared.

Lynda, feeling like Cinderella must have felt after fitting into the glass slipper and flipping the bird to her ugly stepsisters, took two steps towards the kitchen table.

The thin aluminum pie plate collapsed inwards, folding up in half.

Her magnificent creation fell to the floor, splattering in all directions as it hit with a big, wet *splorch*.

The usually-considerate Mark burst into uproarious laughter. (He couldn't help himself; like many males, he was a huge fan of *The Three Stooges*.) He laughed so hard, his face went beet red. Then he saw his partner.

Lynda stood there, stock-still, white-faced, twin bulging tears slithering down her cheeks, staring at the literal fruits of an entire day's labour splashed on the floor like an obscene Rorschach test.

Eager to make amends, ashamed at his gaff, Mark quickly grabbed a fork and vaulted from his chair. Dropping to his knees, he started eating the pie off the floor.

"Mmm, is this ever good!" he gushed. "Nice an' hot, too! Just needs some ice cream - we got any?"

"Wha ... what ARE you doing," she asked, flabbergasted.

"Enjoying your creation! Oh look, here's another part that isn't touching the floor. See? It's so thick, there's lots that isn't actually on the linoleum. Wow, this is really wonderful pie. You sure you've never baked one before? Grab a fork an' dig in, hon! An' when we're done, we'll just let Ferro in here, an' he'll clean up the rest!"

Now it was her turn to laugh and she did so with gusto. The sight of Mark kneeling on the floor wolfing down huge forkfulls of hot strawberry-rhubarb pie was priceless.

"I'm ... I'm gonna do two things," she gasped between giggles, swiping away her tears. "First, take a picture of you eating off the floor. Second, fetch the ice cream from the freezer. You're a big goof, ya know that?"

"Yuph," he said, mouth crammed full.

The things you do for love.

(The next day, they bought a proper, sturdy, glass pie plate. But she hasn't made a pie since. It was also the first and last time they ever had a pig as a house guest. In fact, few humans desired to stay very long in their guest room following Cash's tenancy, which was not necessarily a bad thing.)

"You come to love not by finding the perfect person,
but by seeing an imperfect person perfectly."
– Sam Keen

"All you need is love."
– The Beatles

Rubber Duckies in our (Hot) Tub
Aye, there's the rub (a-dub-dub)

It all started with a single rubber duck. For which I blame my son.

He was away at college in Hamilton some years ago and, during a phone call home, my wife lamented that she had unsuccessfully searched all over town for a cute yellow rubber duck to float in our new backyard hot tub.

Being a dutiful son (and being bored with homework), he jumped on a bus and scoured Steel City, finally bagging a suitably cute floating fowl of lemon hue. On his next visit home, he presented it to her with a grand flourish. My wife gleefully hugged him.

The next time I went out to join her in our spa, a bright yellow interloper was saucily bobbing about with her.

"Um, honey, I thought rubber ducks were a traditional accessory for bathtubs, in the privacy of one's bathroom, safe from the curious eyes of gossipy neigbours," I opined as I slipped into the steaming water.

She splashed me. The duck banged into my face. I'm sure it was merely a coincidence of the swirling currents, but no matter where I moved in the spa, that damned duck found me and attacked.

Both she and my son looked for suitable companions for our solo duck, because, as she rationally pointed out over breakfast one morning, ducks don't swim alone.

However, being a very particular person, she didn't just want other ducks that looked like her first one. I breathed a sigh of relief, since I knew that yellow rubber ducks were mass-produced in vast flocks of identical birds. So I figured I'd only have one bobbing buzzard to contend with in our hot tub.

Then, at a travel trade show in Toronto, at a booth promoting the virtues of visiting Calgary, she saw a cowboy rubber duck as part of their display, complete with hat, bandana and vest. When she left that booth, Cowboy Duck left with her. (No, she didn't steal it; she can be quite persuasive when necessary.)

Some months later, Cowboy Duck was joined by U. S. Air Force Pilot Duck, wearing helmet and goggles, courtesy of the National Museum of the USAF in Dayton, Ohio.

A catalogue hawking British keepsakes yielded a treasure trove of three distinctive English canards: London Bobby, Beefeater Guard, and Buckingham Palace Guard, all in colourful regalia. Oblivious to my groans, they joined our floating flock. Which always persisted in congregating around me as I tried to enjoy our hot tub.

Over the years, many other quackers migrated to our bobbing brood, including Joe Cool Duck sporting suave sunglasses, a glow-in-the-dark Ghost Duck, a groovy purple Flower Power Duck, and Slam Dunk Duck (an orange bird with black stripes shaped like a basketball).

Visiting the King Tut exhibit at the Art Gallery of Ontario in January, 2010, this Egyptian artifact was unearthed in the adjoining Gift Shop: Mummy Duck, swathed in white wrappings with just its eyes, beak, and tail feathers poking out.

It got so bad that one day, as I emerged from the house desperate for a long soothing soak, all I could see was a sea of beaked floating fiends and, almost lost amidst the gaggle, the mischievous eyes and head of my wife.

"Get the flock outta there!" I bellowed. Neighbours, relaxing in their backyards, misheard my words and scolded me for my fowl language.

Things took an irrevocable turn for the worse recently when we patronized the House of Blues restaurant in Downtown Disney, Orlando. In the gift shop, our son (and remember who started all this) discovered two ducks that looked exactly like Jake and Elwood Blues, from the classic *Blues Brothers* movie. They were hatched by a firm called CelebriDucks. When my wife and son checked out their website, it was like Dorothy and her travelling companions seeing the Emerald City for the first time.

Their bedazzled eyes beheld a vast flock of celebrity canards, all available for purchase.

Several weeks later, these famous feathered fowls flew into our spa to nest with Jake and Elwood: Marilyn Monroe, Mr. T, Larry the Cable Guy (complete with "Git-R-Done" ball cap), Michael Jackson in zombie mode from *Thriller*, Gene Simmons as his long-tongued KISS Demon, the Pink Panther, and a horned, red Devil Duck complete with pitchfork ("just who you need when you're in hot water," proclaimed the website).

We're gonna need a much bigger hot tub.

I'm desperately searching for a floating Duck Hunter ...

Lions and Dolphins and Rednecks, Oh My!

Our son works at a national TV network in Toronto; a job that necessitates long commutes. So he has lots of time to think about stuff like this:

Private Security companies you *don't* want to hire.

Phat Boys: They arrive in pimped-out cars and wear floppy clothes with lots of bling. However, they each weigh over 350 pounds. So when a crime occurs, they can't chase anybody. Which is lucky for the perpetrators, because if caught, they get sat upon. Cruel and unusual punishment.

Just Missed 'Em: an agency whose timing is always off. Their logo is a pair of hands grasping at thin air. Perps love this company.

Chalk Outline: A division - and a consequence - of the previous agency. They tend to get fired a lot.

Redneck Security: No joke about these guys. They're lethally efficient, armed and dangerous. Their motto: "Shoot everybody and let God sort 'em out."

Unnecessary Violence: Similar to the previous company, these folks don't know the meaning of restraint. They're hired to tame rough bars, rock concerts, and church rummage sales.

Eye Candy Security: Female agents dress in micro-bikinis, male agents in thongs. In great demand by Hollywood stars, college dorms, and retirement homes.

Clued-Out Security: They look good sitting behind a desk watching TV monitors. But don't ask them to do anything more than that. This agency employs ex-financial advisors, the same people that caused the 2008-2010 worldwide Great Recession.

Non-Violent Politically Correct Agency: Confronted with crime, these folks insist on hosting a group counselling session, to discover the root causes of the thieves' criminal inclinations, and how much blame can be placed upon their parents, society, and unfair media messaging. This procedure results in a 100% conviction record, as the perps desperately desire incarceration to get away from these nuts.

After The Fact: These people are hired by businesses *after* they've had a break-in. It's like implementing spending restraints on bankrupt companies just after top management has awarded themselves huge bonuses. They excel at guarding empty warehouses and almost-worthless stocks.

Cop Wannabes: Police Academy rejects, these would-be officers overindulge in frisking, use of handcuffs, sobriety testing, and looking cool in sunglasses.

Pluto Patrol: Providing security at Walt Disney theme parks, these mutts are on the lookout for anyone not having a good time. Such persons are then bopped on the head and whisked underground to a soundproof room, where they undergo intensive behavior modification from that master of self-control: Donald Duck.

Tarzan Troop: Patrolling the jungle, these apes literally pounce on poachers, smugglers, and tourists who litter or don't stay on the path. Perps have a choice of either listening to a lecture on environmental sustainability, or getting their arms ripped off. Unfortunately, the Troop can be easily bribed with bananas.

Dolphin Dragoons: Seagoing perps are charmed by these agents' perpetually-smiling faces; a fatal mistake. The Dragoons snout-butt the bad guys into unconsciousness, toss them in the air for their own perverse amusement, then leave the battered bodies to the tender mercies of Shark Security.

Sopranos Security: The elite of private security; no thief dares challenge them. Your property and possessions are perfectly safe - until they decide to take it for themselves.

Literary Lions: Composed entirely of frustrated authors needing a steady paycheque "until their big break," these agents subdue perps with witty *bon mots* and withering sarcasm. If that fails, they lull criminals to sleep by reading from their unpublished works (a fate worse than death). Their life expectancy is three days.

Conventional Wisdom
meets Unconventional Reality
Beware The Glare

A customary part of the job description for people who run non-profit organizations for a living, like I do, is the requirement to organize and deliver your association's annual convention. If we do our jobs right, our delegates have an energizing, educational, worthwhile convention experience. However, to compensate for all the stress and strain we endure when putting on these events, we association managers often need a hefty dose of well-lubricated R & R immediately afterwards. Why?

Because at one time or another in our professional careers, we've had to deal with situations like these:

A wildcat labour strike hits your host hotel one week before your convention starts, and the hotel's iron-clad 185-page contract that you nervously signed months ago absolves them from any blame or remedial action whatsoever. When you inquire if the strike might be settled soon, you're told the employees are constructing benches cemented into the sidewalk, with awnings for summer and heaters for winter, and a fast-food restaurant is being built immediately adjacent.

Just as bad: Your convention's official airline, charged with flying in delegates from across the country, that insisted on fully pre-paid non-refundable tickets to obtain their low convention fare, abruptly goes bankrupt two days before your event starts.

Key staffers getting horribly sick the day before the convention, breaking the cardinal rule in their employment contract that staff are forbidden to become ill until the event is over.

Your convention program is printed and proudly placed in every one of 500 delegate's kits. You arrive at the hotel, only to discover they have switched all the meeting rooms. ("Oh, didn't you get the email?") Despite signage to redirect the herd, some of your delegates spend hours listening to another convention's completely-unrelated speakers, nodding wisely and taking notes.

Others get lost in the labyrinth of the hotel for days.

Your keynote speaker has been re-confirmed so many times that he/she is on your phone's speed-dial and his/her Significant Other recognizes your voice when you call. He/she still shows up late. There's nothing quite like The Glare a Chairperson gives you when you inform them that they have to "keep the audience engaged" for 30 or 45 minutes until SuperStar finally deigns to show up.

One panellist on your hand-picked panel of experts, all coached months beforehand and thoroughly briefed on your audience, sends a last-minute substitute; someone who obviously drew the short straw at the office, who is clearly unprepared and totally uninterested. The Chairperson drills you with The Glare.

Delegates who treat the host bar as if it was a bottomless well - and are determined to empty that well no matter what it takes.

A highly-recommended busker entertaining your delegates with a heart-stopping display of sword juggling, who nicks himself with his own sword. Then ignores the blood slowly spreading across his white silk shirt and insists on juggling even larger swords - with your incoming Chairperson rigidly standing right in front of him. Said Chairperson-elect bestowing The Glare upon you, while silently mouthing The Lord's Prayer (and she's not even Christian).

An after-dinner comedian who's so drunk and so insulting that half the audience walks out - and those remaining ask for extra bread rolls to lob at the jerk.

At least the comedian showed up. What's worse is having your post-banquet entertainment cancel abruptly, blaming a blizzard so fierce that small cars are being swallowed by snow drifts, never to be seen until Spring. (You're positive it's a lie, although you haven't seen the outside of the hotel in four days.)

So your Chairperson gives you The Glare, and insists that *you* entertain the troops yourself, with no prep time nor props nor costume. What you end up doing is so embarrassing that you intend to resign that very evening, yet the delegates roar with laughter and so you don't feel too bad.

Then you discover that your ever-alert staff took digital photos, which they lovingly post on your association's website the next morning.

True story: A middle-aged Chairperson and his middle-aged wife arrive at the closing banquet so pre-lubricated that they can hardly walk straight, continue drinking through dinner, then announce an impromptu fund-raiser for the local children's hospital; said funds to be raised by delegates throwing money on stage as the royal couple perform a slow, ghastly strip tease. (I always wondered at the morbid fascination people get from watching a train wreck. Now I know.)

A Chairperson who completely ignores the script that you fretted over for hours, because he/she believes it will sound "more natural" if they ad-lib it (also believing they are the next Leno or Letterman, just waiting to be discovered). When it finally becomes obvious to them that they've totally lost the audience, in no small part because of their tasteless jokes, they then wave the script in the air and announce you as the author.

Afternoon sessions that take on an immortal life of their own and, despite your best efforts, run long past their time limit, causing the evening dinner to be so late that the promised juicy prime rib comes out looking like dry shoe leather and tasting much worse. And you dare not blame the chef - such persons carry a large knife and know how to use it.

A delegate who has the temerity to disrupt your perfectly-planned Welcome Reception by having a heart attack. And the EMS personnel go to the wrong room, insisting on resuscitating someone who just had too much to drink.

A fire alarm that erupts just as the Honourable Cabinet Minister, who you've worked for months to get to your convention, announces to your packed audience major new funding for your industry sector. The alarm, blasting enough decibels to deafen a heavy metal rocker, continues so that it cannot be ignored and, dammit, all of you must evacuate to the outside. (It's February in Winnipeg and it's 30 degrees below zero; 50 below with the wind chill.) Of course, it's a false alarm.

You get a frozen Glare from both the Chairperson and the Honourable Minister.

However, if the gods smile upon you and all goes well, so that you and your staff team deliver a flawless convention praised by delegates as the best ever, savor the moment, pilgrim, for it will be fleeting. After it's over, none of your directors will send you flowers, chocolates, or even notes of thanks. At the next Board meeting, they will pontificate at tedious length on what could have been done better.

And that's why, when I started in this career 30 years ago, I had a full head of hair ...

I've discovered that spouses have also perfected The Glare. Oy.

76 Skeleton Bones in the Big Parade

One thing kids love is dressing up for Hallowe'en. Whether pirate or princess, ghost or goblin, superhero or slimeball, youngsters eagerly assume alter egos in their quest for candy.

It's a scientific fact that the youthful urge to wear costumes survives into adulthood. How else to explain garish fans at sports events and Jimmy Buffett concerts?

In the 1970s, as newlyweds, we discovered that Rutland, Vermont, a quaint town nestled among the Green Mountains, hosted an annual Hallowe'en Parade themed around superheroes. A great boost to tourism, it attracted folks from near and far, either to ride a float dressed as a defender (or nemesis) of truth and justice, or to watch. Deciding this was something we just had to do, we designed two barbarian costumes, inspired by the *Conan the Barbarian* comic book and, later, two movies starring California's future Governator. (With our sewing skills, such costumes were easier to make than something in colourful spandex.)

Acquiring some grey faux fur, we made a loincloth for me and a bikini for her, to wear over our bathing suits. We created long cloaks out of crushed velvet, orange for her, deep purple for me (barbarians having atrocious fashion sense). To accessorize our outfits, I constructed a spear and shield for my heathen honey and swiped my parents' 19th century heirloom sword for myself.

Off we drove to Rutland.

The U.S. border guards took one look at the weapons in our car and promptly pulled us aside for some serious questioning. Eventually reassured that we weren't the vanguard of a Canadian force attempting to retake Her Majesty's former colonies, they let us enter. (Nowadays, with post-9/11 paranoia, our Weapons of Mass Destruction would have been impounded, with us winning an all-expense-paid trip to a scenic bay in Cuba.)

Arriving in Rutland, we checked into an historic downtown

hotel. Night fell, and heroes and villains of every size, shape and colour emerged from secret lairs and clambered onto a convoy of floats. We encountered two unforseen problems. One: At the end of October, at night, it was too cold for skimpily-clad barbarians, no matter how ferocious we looked. Two: The parade organizers didn't know where to place two Canucks wearing hastily-purchased "Rutland" sweatshirts under their barbaric ensembles. We didn't fit the superhero theme.

Finally relegated to a float of "miscellaneous" characters (*Star Trek* aliens, sorcerers, warrior nuns, elves, trolls, a lawyer), we had a great time as the parade wound through the town full of cheering throngs. Afterwards, Conan declared a mighty hunger and demanded a fatted calf be slaughtered, accompanied by lusty buxom wenches serving frothing flagons of ale.

We went to McDonald's.

As we entered in full regalia, carrying spear and sword, the staff freaked. Relieved we weren't there to loot and pillage, the manager graciously comped our meals.

Although our home town of Peterborough is already blessed with several annual parades, my wife had the inspiration that we could also do with a Hallowe'en Parade. Floats would carry creatures of the night, swashbucklers, superheroes, movie characters, and aliens, with appropriate music blaring, like *Thriller, Monster Mash,* and *Ghostbusters.*

Businesses normally left out of sponsoring parade floats could participate, such as funeral parlours, cemeteries, crematoriums, morticians, monument carvers, and the Amalgamated Gravediggers Union, Local 666.

The biggest problem? Hardly anyone would line our main street to gawk; everyone would want to ride a float in costume!

So why doesn't someone organize a Hallowe'en Parade in Peterborough? We still have our barbarian costumes. Though the fur doesn't quite cover what it used to. Maybe it shrunk?

I often wonder why wearing swords went out of fashion. Ditto crushed velvet.

Timing is Everything

About a year ago, our trusty, carefully-maintained elderly washing machine decided it finally had enough of us and committed suicide.

We trooped into our friendly neighbourhood appliance store and purchased a new one, after I first failed to convince my wife that it would be more eco-friendly to hire a young Filipino woman to live with us and do our laundry by hand using an antique scrub board. Mechanically, our new clothes washer worked great. However ...

Several months later, we noticed a smell in our laundry room. It was a stale, musty odour which, after burning my old high school gym socks (a treasured heirloom), we finally traced to our new washing machine.

A yellowing advice column clipped from our local newspaper was unearthed. It described how to get rid of stale washer odours, although such fragrances were only supposed to happen after years of use.

I faithfully followed the instructions, which involved overfilling the tub with hot water, adding several cups of bleach, and sacrificing a silk blouse to Tide, the ancient Greek god of laundry.

The smell persisted. So I repeated the cleansing process, this time sacrificing a cold beer to Tide, in hopes my prayer would be answered.

The machine still stunk. In fact, the stink got worse. It permeated the entire house, raising suspicions among visitors about our housecleaning hygiene.

My wife called the manufacturer's Customer Care Hotline. Turned out the line was more lukewarm than hot, as it took her forever to connect with a live body. An expert was eventually exhumed, who outlined a procedure to banish our pungent perfume.

It was the exact same procedure I had already followed - twice - from the newspaper clipping.

She then arranged a service call. The rep, with much grunting and muttering, dismantled our entire machine, looking for mold, soap build-up, dead mice, or the neighbour's missing cat.

He found nothing.

He graced us with a stiff bill for a Frivolous Service Call, something deeply frowned-upon by the company.

Then our son had a Bright Idea (he gets that from my side of the family). He theorized the noisome aroma could be caused by stagnant water trapped in the corrugations of the machine's drainage hose.

He devised an elaborate method of checking his theory. He would hold the hose upright as the machine washed a load. Then, mere seconds before the machine discharged its tub full of water, he would swiftly pour a quart of undiluted chlorine bleach down the hose, then place the hose in the laundry sink just before the machine spewed forth. The hose would thus receive a bleach bath.

The gap between theory and practice is often deeper than the Grand Canyon.

After carefully timing the washing cycle, our college graduate held the hose upright, gingerly funneled in the bleach, and was just lowering the hose towards the sink when the machine abruptly vomited like a frat boy after an all-night bender.

A hoseful of concentrated bleach struck him full in the chest, chased by a tubful of cold water. Which was quite provident, since the water diluted the bleach, preventing a skin burn. However, the chemical did leave a ginormous white scar on his favorite black golf shirt.

We thanked our son for his clever idea and made a mental note to get him a more accurate watch for Christmas.

My legendary patience was exhausted; I'd had enough of newspaper tips, manufacturer's advice, and ideas from our soaking-wet offspring. I resolved to fix our odorous washer my way.

Did you know that hardware stores have a marvellous selection of sledgehammers?

Your author certifies that no soaking-wet offspring was permanently harmed in the creation of this story.

Fast Food Follies

My first job after graduating from McGill University in Montreal with an honours degree in education and glowing recommendations about what a gifted high school teacher I would be, was as a restaurant manager for an internationally-famous hamburger chain. Go figure. I was rotated through several of their stores in Quebec and Ontario, my last posting being at a store in Hamilton.

Just over 20 years later, my son's part-time job while away at college in Hamilton was working as a crew member for the same internationally-famous hamburger chain, albeit at a different store. Sheer coincidence, or genetics? Do you want fries with that?

Besides our dashing good looks and skill at avoiding household chores, among the other things my son and I have in common are stories from our respective fast food days. Stories like these:

On rare occasions, customers would return to the front counter complaining that the burger they'd ordered was not what they'd unwrapped at their tables. Naively believing that the customer is always right, I cheerfully swapped the offending sandwich with a fresh one made to the customer's specifications.

One day, a burly man thumped the counter, thus getting my attention, and loudly complained that his burger had mustard on it, yet he had distinctly ordered no mustard because he *hated* mustard. The burger was half-eaten. Assuring him that he'd promptly receive a new burger, I held out my hand to receive the partly-devoured imperfect one. Whereupon he took one last huge bite of the sandwich, stuffing his mouth to bursting and, mustard dripping from his lower lip, handed me the almost-extinct remains.

Another time, late at night, my female crew person at the pick-up window was startled to see three young men stumble up to the drive-through speaker. One actually careened into the pole holding the speaker, hitting it hard enough to shake it, before collapsing in a heap at its base.

She called me over to deal with this, just as one guy slurred their order into the microphone. I told them over the speaker that we had a policy of only serving people in cars at the drive-through, for our own safety and security.

Came his reply: "But we're too damn drunk to drive! Ya don't want us behind the wheel in our condition, do ya?"

I certainly did not, and I certainly did not want them staggering into my restaurant to eat here either. I quickly waived the policy and agreed to serve them through the pick-up window. En route from mike to window, one of the trio showed his appreciation by vomiting into our flower bed.

I was often the only male present during openings in the mornings, which meant it was my enviable task to carry the heavy pot of hot chili from stove to sink, and upend it over the edge of the deep sink to pour its steaming contents into a bin, placed there beforehand, which would then be carried out to the front counter to serve customers. This was decades before today's health and safety regulations of wearing enough protective gear to qualify as a Hazmat technician: thick rubberized chest-high apron, insulated gloves that come almost up to your shoulder, and a full-face protective shield. Back then, crew in general and managers in particular were apparently more expendable; all we had were short gloves and an admonition to be careful.

I picked up the tall, wide stainless steel pot by its side handles, as I had done hundreds of times before, and carried it to the sink. As I raised it up, the bottom of the pot hit the edge of the sink and the pot tipped backwards. Onto me.

I was doused with scalding chili, which quickly soaked through both my thin white chest-high apron and blue-and-white striped shirt, to my skin. I was splashed from chest to upper thighs, as the hot stuff also soaked my trousers. In those days, managers wore white trousers.

Manfully stifling a cry of pain, I poured what was left of the pot into the chili bin in the sink, then walked out to the front to see if the chili station was ready to receive the bin. It was fortunate we weren't open yet. The two college coeds readying the sandwich station and front counter took one look at my gory red clothes and shrieked. They immediately assumed I had been mortally wounded by a knife-wielding maniac in the kitchen, and that they were the obvious next targets. I told them what happened and their shrieks transformed into gales of laughter. Very compassionate.

I beat a hasty retreat to the male washroom. I had a spare shirt and apron, but no pants. To hide my red-splattered pants front, I broke dress code and wore a half-apron for the rest of the day. I also had to endure interminable female giggles.

Some months later, on my last day at that job prior to starting a new career in association management, my crew gave me a farewell dinner. There was something that had been puzzling me for months, and I decided to finally clear it up.

Of my regular crew of sandwich-makers, one twentysomething woman was the shining star. No one else could make a sandwich faster than she, and she was always 100% accurate too. She was sitting next to me, so I asked:

"Tell me, Karen, what is your secret? How can you make sandwiches so fast and so accurately, every single day you work here?"

Karen smiled and took a long sip of her drink. Then she brushed back a strand of her long blonde hair, leaned close to me, and murmured:

"I'm stoned."

"What!?" I blurted.

"Yeppir," she laughed. "I always toke up before I come on duty. I mean, don't get me wrong; you're a great boss, but I couldn't get through my shift otherwise."

That was something I never found under "Helpful Hints to Improve Employee Productivity" in the chain's Operations Manual.

Over two decades later, my son was working the sandwich station on the night shift. When closing time loomed, the crew started cleaning up their stations. Five minutes before closing, the thing that closing crews hate occurred: a hungry couple entered. They ordered two fried chicken sandwiches. Tony, my son's co-worker, was in charge of the grill and the deep fryers. He blanched.

"I don't have anything ready!" He scampered into the walk-in freezer and emerged with two frozen chicken breasts, caked with ice. In full view of the couple, he started vigorously banging the meat hard against the outside of the fryer, to shake loose the ice, since water and fry oil got along about the same as classical music lovers and rap afficionados.

WHAM! WHAM! WHAM! went the chicken as the couple watched, aghast.

"Ah, I hope to God that's not our food," said the man.

"Oh no, no," replied the cashier smoothly. "That's extra, in case someone else comes in. Yours is already cooking. Now why don't you go sit down in the dining room and I'll bring you your food when it's ready."

As the couple moved off, the cashier looked at the chicken-banger, then at my son, and they all smirked.

Tony said that was as much ice gone as was going to go. He stepped back from the fryer and gingerly slid the frozen chicken breasts into the hot oil. It immediately started seething and bubbling, like a lab experiment about to explode. Loud pops filled the air. Tony quickly moved to stand beside my son, many feet away.

"And that's why you don't mix water with Frymax," he announced solemnly.

"Thanks for the important safety tip," said my son, watching the churning fryer, wide-eyed.

My son and his colleagues had to endure a co-worker who very obviously loathed showers. When this guy came on duty, his intense body odour made everyone else almost physically ill as he walked past them to his station at the grill. This, despite his liberal doses of cheap cologne.

Hours later, even through the heavy smells of cooking meat and grease, his B.O. was still nauseatingly apparent. The other crew spoke to the manager about him, but skilled grill persons were worth their weight in cheap cologne, so she did nothing.

When "The Skunk" was on duty, my son always ate at a neighbouring restaurant on his lunch break.

Ever-mindful of keeping the "fast" in "food," the restaurant chain had timers that measured how long it took to serve a customer at the drive-through windows. Activated when the cashier punched in an order from the speaker, the timer ticked away between the first window, where customers paid for their order, and the second window, where they received their bagged feast. Store managers were obsessed with serving within the mandated times, since slow service looked bad on their performance reports. However, during very busy periods, despite everyone's best efforts, things sometimes got bogged down and the service exceeded the prescribed times.

That's when the manager at my son's store got creative.

Around 10:30 one night, after a busy day when the drive-through times were above the ordained standard, the manager took the handcart that was used to move heavy boxes of meat and produce, and went to the first pick-up window. She keyed-in an order of tap water at the cash, a no-charge order. Then she opened the window and, as my astonished son watched from his position at the grill, flung the handcart through it. *Thump, thump, thump, WHRANG!* The heavy dolly bounced down the exterior wall bricks on its rubber wheels and its thick steel bottom plate slammed onto the concrete pressure plate on the ground beneath the window.

She then hauled the handcart back up the wall, its tires again bouncing along the bricks, and in through the window. She raced to the second window, yanked it open and, heaving the dolly outside, repeated the process. *Thump, thump, thump, WHRANG!*

She performed the whole procedure about six times. Finally, panting, she closed both windows and returned the handcart to the storage room.

"Ah, what was that all about?" asked my son warily, wondering if he should have somehow pried more money out of his tightwad parents instead of taking that part-time job.

"It lowers the average drive-through times for the day by

tricking the system into thinking we had more cars than we actually had," she replied. "And you never saw what you just saw, got it?"

"Got it. Um, wouldn't it be a lot less hassle if you just drove over the pressure plates with your car?"

"Don't have a car, genius. I believe in public transit. Save the planet."

She saw the look my son gave her and sighed. "Okay, it's 'cause I can't afford a car right now. Now clean your grill."

Some weeks later, once again on the night closing shift, my son was being trained in the fine art of proper floor cleaning. Sally, the store's designated trainer, was in a foul mood, caused by equal parts dislike at the chore of training and the cosmic injustice of having to work for a living.

"Just put the cleaning solution into the bucket, wet the floor with it, and mop," was the extent of Sally's expert instruction. Then she disappeared into the manager's office to spend time with her girlfriend.

Parts of a restaurant's tiled kitchen floor get quite greasy after a long day. My son, eager to please, figured he'd "amp up" the standard cleaning solution. To the usual Mr. Clean floor cleaner, he added healthy doses of degreaser, bleach, and other chemicals he found on the cleaning shelf. He created his own blend of secret herbs 'n' spices, producing a frothy concoction guaranteed to cut through anything on that floor. (Possibly including the tiles.)

He wet down the entire kitchen and staff room area. However, his second pass with fresh water and mop, intended to dry the glistening floor, was forestalled when a big group of late-night customers came in. As per the store's operating policy, he abandoned his cleaning to return to his scheduled post at the grill. His cursory floor cleaning training had omitted the health and safety directive to place the bright yellow "Caution Wet Floor" signs in the affected area.

Alerted that a sudden rush of people had arrived and that the sandwich station needed an extra pair of hands, Sally emerged from the manager's back office and raced to the front counter.

Right through the slick, wet floor.

My son and his co-workers heard a surprised scream. From his station at the grill, my son whipped his head around in time to see Sally shoot down the floor on her back and slam into the stove with a mighty crash. This collision prompted a chorus of shouted invective that turned the air blue and would have made truck drivers and stevedores blush crimson.

The customers heard every word.

"Why the damn HELL is the damn floor so wet? And what the damn HELL is on it? It's so damn slippery!" she yelled, limping into the front area. (To protect sensitive readers, I've substituted the word "damn" for the far more colourful and descriptive words she used.)

"I was cleaning it, of course," replied my son, concerned that he might be attacked and grateful there were witnesses. "But I had to stop to come out here to serve these customers."

"Well, did you have to wet the WHOLE damn floor? I fell on my damn ass and slid right into the damn stove! My damn shin smashed into the damn stove leg!"

"Well, Sally, it seems that you didn't do a very good job of training him then, eh?" opined the guy at the sandwich station. My son and the cashier chortled.

Sally flushed angrily. She opened her mouth to fire a withering broadside when she noticed the big line of customers gawking at her. She forced a broad smile, turned on her heel, and limped off into the back of the store.

All three front line crew dissolved into helpless laughter, not just at Sally's spectacular crash, but at the poetic justice of the so-called trainer falling prey to her own incompetence.

To this day, despite an intimate knowledge of what goes on behind the front counter, my son and I still patronize this fast food chain. That's because the stories we heard about what goes on at the OTHER chains are even worse.

Mothballed Hero

The middle-aged former superhero turned away from the window with a heavy sigh. It had been years since that distinctive signal had stabbed the night sky, summoning the Dark Avenger. Nowadays, thanks to budget cuts, the police rented the rooftop searchlight to a strip club. That certainly was no Dark Avenger symbol shining on the clouds tonight.

He just wasn't needed anymore. After he'd captured all the weirdos, psychos and perverts that comprised his Rogues' Gallery, he'd been reduced to nabbing jaywalkers and citizens who let their cars idle too long.

With the writing on the wall (and he'd busted those graffiti artists too), he'd reluctantly hung up his cape and retired.

That had been some years ago. He was now completely *bored*. There were only so many times he could haunt his vast Trophy Room, and reminisce over a beer with the Human Cockroach (also retired).

Adrenaline suddenly surged through him. *Enough moping!* He'd go out on patrol again! Tonight!

He squeezed through the secret entrance in the mansion's library (*was it always that tight?*) and descended the cobwebbed stairs to his cave lair. He hit the lights. Several bulbs blew. Other lights only flickered weakly.

He wiped the dust off the plexiglass display case and eyed his imposing outfit. Pride swelled within him: *The dreaded Dark Avenger would prowl again!*

He started donning the uniform. The pants stretched dangerously over his butt (*material must've shrunk*). When he bent to put on his boots, he felt the rear pants seam split. (*The cape will cover it.*)

The only way he could get the armored vest to fit, was to suck in his stomach. When he exhaled, the vest creaked alarmingly. A rivet suddenly popped and skittered across the dank floor.

There was no way he could buckle his utility belt.

As he fumbled with the clasps that attached his cape, he glanced at the familiar red-yellow-green outfit in the adjoining display case. Yeah, his little bird had grown up long ago. The brat had decided there was a better way to fight crime: he became a federal politician and got stiff gun-control laws passed. It worked too: gun crime was way down among honest citizens. Meanwhile, gang shootings soared.

The Dark Avenger strode to the long tarpaulin-shrouded shape in the centre of the cave. Grunting with exertion, he pulled off the heavy guano-splattered canvas.

The sleek ebony vehicle gleamed in the fitful light. (*You want to get out there as badly as I do, don't you, Matilda?*)

He slid behind the steering wheel, which pressed into his bulging abdomen. His thighs overflowed the bucket seat. The racing harness strained to buckle shut.

He pushed buttons and flipped switches. The mighty turbine spooled into life. The car thrummed with power. When all (*okay, most*) lights glowed green on the dash, he pressed the accelerator while keeping the brake engaged. The engine screamed its familiar wail and he released the brake. The black beast shot forward as he yanked the lever to raise the camouflaged cave wall.

"Yeee-HAH!" he shouted.

With an agonizing screech, the turbine seized. Good thing too. The mechanism that lifted the cave wall was rusted solid.

The car still had enough momentum to crash into the wall. Our hero's face smashed into the steering wheel as the air bag failed to deploy.

"The hell with this," the Dark Avenger muttered as he used his cape to swab blood from his face. "I'm gonna call my old Justice Syndicate buddies for a game of euchre. The Purple Porpoise still owes me twenty bucks."

Your author, also middle-aged, likewise rarely patrols in costume anymore.

Alphabet Soup

There seems to be an ever-increasing number of people staunchly opposed to change. Perhaps it's yet another effect of global warming. Tom McLaren, in an article published in the June, 2008, *Association* magazine, described several acronyms depicting the change-phobic. The first one is fairly well-known:

NIMBY: Not In My Back Yard. NIMBYs exist everywhere, though Toronto seems to be the Canadian epicentre, according to a February, 2008, *Toronto Star* article.

But the number of other acronyms surprised me; I had no idea NIMBYs had so many close relatives:

BANANA: Build Absolutely Nothing Anywhere Near Anybody. BANANAs support new projects in principle, provided that the projects are located away from people and certainly not near them. I guess suitable building sites would include Antarctica, Siberia, the Mariana Trench at the bottom of the Pacific Ocean, and Moncton.

GOMBY: Get Out of My Back Yard. GOMBYs live in neighbourhoods with an existing unwanted land use, like strip mining or a children's daycare. Which begs the question: Didn't they know this before moving in?

CAVE: Citizens Against Virtually Everything. Sometimes called CAVE people, these neanderthals see the world only one way - theirs - and refuse to change their minds. Their best buddies are:

NOPE: Not On Planet Earth. The NOPE crowd thinks the Moon is an excellent location for new development. They also heartily support NASA's planned colonization of Mars.

And lest you think this is all one-sided, Mr. McLaren also describes:

DUDE: Developer Under Delusions of Entitlement. DUDEs believe that community consultation and engagement is not their responsibility. When finally shamed into holding meetings with stakeholders, it's long after decisions have been made, plans have been finalized, the authorities' approval has been secured, and photo-ops with beaming politicians have been staged.

That article makes some thought-provoking points. However, I think it doesn't go far enough. I humbly present these kindred spirits:

NUTS: Never Understand The Situation. Their motto explains it all: "Don't confuse me with facts; my mind is made up."

PIP: Politically Incorrect People. PIPs are fed up with all the cautious, expensive political correctness stifling modern society. They yearn for days past when Chairpersons were Chairmen, gay meant merry or festive, and Christmas trees were everywhere.

GOOFY: Group Obstinately Opposed to Flying Year-round. Fanatically concerned with carbon footprints, they have singled out airplanes as leaving the biggest: a size 24 in a size 8 world. GOOFY believes hot air balloons, fueled by politicians' hot air, are a viable alternative, using a renewable resource.

Then there's these socially-significant groups:

TWITS: Teenagers With Ingrained Teen Superiority. Believing that anyone over the age of 20 is hopelessly clued-out and impossibly old, TWITS celebrate the fact that mass-market advertisers, movies, music, TV shows, and clothes pander to their age group. They're convinced that acne was secretly created by vindictive adults failing to look cool in teen-inspired fashions.

DEAD: Devotees of Entrees, Appetizers and Desserts. The grateful DEAD love food: all types, colours, shapes and sizes. They live to eat. Chowing down is the highlight of their day; they even plan vacations around great restaurants (it's called Culinary Tourism). Their nemesis is:

DIET: Deny Interesting and Exciting Trappings. Followers of DIET believe tofu is the most exciting edible concoction ever, closely followed by lettuce, bean sprouts, alfalfa and kumquats. All washed down with a glass of clearish, thrice-filtered, never-bottled tap water. Yummy.

DORK: Dads Overwhelmed by Rambunctious Kids. DORKs

valiantly ride herd on their little monsters, stifling the urge to euthanize them, while counting the minutes before Mom returns.

MORK: Mothers Overwhelmed by Rambunctious Kids. Same as above, but with genders reversed.

WIMP: Writers Intending to Make a Profit. While most authors suffer from delusions of someday making a living at their craft, WIMPs are those misguided souls who have self-published their books, being rewarded with expenses as long as their arm and revenue as long as their thumb.

Allegations that your author is a DEAD WIMP are unproven; however, he's never met an acronym he didn't like.

The Oddball Olympics

Bad enough that golf and ballroom dancing are being seriously considered for Olympic events. Now we have a group pushing to get pole dancing into the Olympics. *Pole dancing!* How could that ever be taken seriously, in the same Olympic telecast as swimming, cycling, gymnastics, and street protests? Would reporting on pole dancing go into the Sports section of the paper, or in Entertainment? (The Classifieds, next to "Escorts"?) Besides, they already use poles at the Olympics; athletes vault with them.

Oh wait, now I get it: pole dancing would be another excuse to force female contestants to wear skimpy outfits, like the micro-bikinis in women's beach volleyball (easy to see why the mostly-male International Olympic Committee approved *that* sport).

Well, in the spirit of oddball "sports" clamoring to become Olympic events, I humbly suggest the following athletic activities also be seriously considered:

Lap Dancing. A natural complement to pole dancing. Actually, the same skilled athletes could compete in both. ("Judges, please be seated ...")

Jaywalking. Undeniably athletic, especially across busy thoroughfares. The ultimate contact sport, when vehicles hit unlucky contestants. Would be the only Olympic sport that players could easily practice while holding down regular jobs, meaning no fundraisers or government support needed. Athletes would jaywalk to and from work, on their breaks, their lunch hours, and in the evenings. (Weekends would be spent visiting fellow jaywalkers in hospital.)

Shopping Frenzy. A demanding sport with lots of sweating, swearing and savvy outmaneuvering, plus endurance (lining up for hours overnight to be among the first ten doorcrashers), and strength (grabbing the item you want away from an opponent). And that's just the men at electronics sales. It gets downright nasty with women at clothing sales.

Frisbee Tossing. Frisbee Golf and the Ultimate Frisbee team sport are already popular. There would be an Olympic twist: human-dog teams. Why not dogs? They're very entertaining when leaping up to catch frisbees (especially in slow-motion replay on TV), and the Olympics already allow humans and horses to team up for equestrian events. The winning mutt would get a small Olympic medal for their dog collar, matching the larger one given their master. Points deducted for failing to poop 'n' scoop, and growling at the judges.

Competitive Gorging. Male and female athletes would race against the clock, gorging themselves on hot dogs, pancakes, pies, and slurpees. Plus our uniquely Canadian contribution to the sport: poutine gorging! It would all be grossly telegenic, but hey, so is boxing and they give out Olympic medals for that. Gorging is already a serious event at country fairs. And continuing the country theme:

Cow Tipping. Athletes would be scored on the fastest tip, heaviest cow, most surprised cow. Any "cow patties" stepped in reduces the score.

Rodeo Sports. Already popular on TV with millions of viewers, so why not award Olympic medals to the best in bareback riding, saddle-bronc riding, bull riding, barrel racing, calf roping, chuck wagon racing and ten-gallon hat throwing?

Pit Spitting. Another big hit at country fairs. Would have different degrees of difficulty depending on the type of pits: date, cherry, Brad. This event and the previous three would attract that lucrative Western-wannabe demographic. Yee-Haw!

Food Fighting. Athletes judged for number of hits on opponents and types of food used. The messier the missile, the higher the score. Extra points for technique in throwing. Splattering the judges means instant disqualification.

Mall Walking. Finally! An Olympic event for seniors!

Darts. The staple pastime of pubs worldwide, with millions of athletes already skilled and raring to go, so no government funding would be needed for this sport either.

Billiards. The Olympics consider ping pong ... er, table tennis ... and badminton serious medal sports, so why not billiards? Because of those aforementioned pubs and bars, there's legions of squinty-eyed trained athletes with chalked pool cues at the ready.

Square, Line, Scottish, English Country, Jazz, Polka, Ballet, Flamenco and Street Dancing. Also Riverdancing and Flashdancing. Once they let ballroom dancing in, afficionados of other dance styles would twist, twirl, stomp, high-kick, leap, and swing their partner until the IOC lets them do-si-do for a medal too.

Skydiving. Athletes would be judged on types and complexity of group formations, colourful outfits, and closeness to earth before pulling chutes. Going *splat* results in permanent disqualification. Judges must jump with the skydivers to properly assess them, as must the TV camerapeople. (That screaming you hear is not the athletes.)

Potato Peeling. Here again we already have hordes of well-trained athletes in their prime: military personnel. This would turn one of the military's least-liked chores into a shot at Olympic glory. Imagine the boost to morale! Imagine the fresh-cut fries served in the Olympic Village! Hoo-Rah!

Fishing. If the IOC finds golf entertaining, then fishing is a shoe-in. Athletes would be judged not only on number, type and size of fish caught, but how long they can sit motionless and still stay awake. At the Winter Olympics, it would be ice fishing, of course. Both would be a challenging Olympic sport, as beer-drinking would not be allowed while competing. Speaking of Canada's national drink:

Beer Chugging. Party animals worldwide would line up to compete. Normally, Canada and Germany would be the powerhouses to beat. But they'd be at a disadvantage, since the beer would have to be non-alcoholic, because of the Olympics' anti-drug rules. Besides, alcoholic beer would preclude Israel and Muslim countries from competing, and the IOC would want to avoid those protests (and the subsequent loss of TV revenue).

Sheep Shearing. Remove the wool from your eyes; it's not such a baa-ad idea, ewe know. The by-product of this sport would be used for:

Knitting & Rug Hooking. Two more sports perfect for older athletes.

Chess & Checkers. Absolutely riveting sports. Would give golf a run for its money. Contestants would get in shape by eating lots of fish ("brain food"), and practicing intense stares sitting hunched forward for hours.

Video Gaming. Would attract a whole new demographic to participate in, and watch, the Olympics. There's already a host of obsessed, skilled video game players out there. No government funding necessary; the immensely-wealthy video game manufacturers would sponsor top players. An expert TV commentator would translate "game-speak" into English.

Gardening. Easily as engrossing to watch on TV as golf and curling. Those who claim that gardening is not an athletic activity, have never spent hours bent over in the hot sun deweeding, or carrying heavy bags of fertilizer, or hauling wheelbarrowfulls of earth, or chasing varmints from vegetables and flowers.

Snowshoeing. Hey, they let in cross-country skiing, but they completely ignored its bigfooted cousin. Unfair! And once snowshoeing gets in, how about:

Tobogganing. Not the sleek, high-tech, evolved version (bobsledding), but the good old-fashioned traditional version: long wooden toboggans, families of four, smallest kid in the front, snow in everyone's faces, impossible to steer, screaming all the way down until they hit that tree ...

Bull Running. Why should folks who've temporarily taken leave of their senses in Spain have all the fun? Make the Running of the Bulls an Olympic sport and let the whole world share! Medals would be awarded to runners who escape being gored and, because the Olympics are all about fairness, to bulls that gore the *loco* humans.

Ultimate Fighting Championship. Making bloodthirsty, vicious mixed martial arts competitions an Olympic event would lock in that sport's prized young male demographic; great news for ticket sales and TV ad revenue. A natural complement to other violent Olympic sports like boxing, hockey, bobsledding, and ticket-scalping.

Poker, Euchre, Crazy Eights, Old Maid, Go Fish, Bridge, and other card games. Poker is a given, as Championship Poker is already a hit on TV. Once they let that in, then players of all other types of card games would demand to be dealt in too. Especially for Strip Poker. Which naturally leads me to:

Sex. The ultimate Olympic pairs competition. Heck, they're halfway there with pairs figure skating routines. Athletes would be judged on technique, endurance, and inventiveness. (Hugh Hefner would be Judge Emeritus.) Well-suited to ex-curlers ("Hurry! Hurry HARD!"). The IOC would make a fortune on the TV bidding rights. Serious problem to overcome: where would the number and national flag of each athelete go?

Anyone thinking that last suggestion is too off-the-wall, should remember that the ancient Greeks competed in their Olympic Games in the nude. Now wouldn't *that* send TV ratings through the roof!

Unfortunately, if all these sensible suggestions were adopted, the Olympics would last for three months, diverting billions of dollars of TV advertising revenue away from vital programming, thus jeopardizing reality shows, daytime soaps, game shows, WWE wrestling, talk shows, and the breathless reporting of all-news channels.

The very fabric of modern society would unravel.

My favorite athletic activity is swinging in a hammock, but the chances of that becoming an Olympic event are rather slim. For now.

Pusser's Pirates
Yo Ho Ho and a Painkiller with Pizza

Tendrils of early-morning mist slowly melted away from the verdant British Virgin Islands as the tropical sun broached the horizon. Wraith-quiet, the ebony hull of the pirate raider sliced through the azure Caribbean toward Roadtown, Tortola.

Aboard ship, the battle-hardened crew licked their parched lips. Soon, they would quench their thirst with the best grog this side of heaven.

Slipping through Roadtown's harbour, heedless of the floating corpses of cruise ship passengers fallen overboard in drunken stupors, the dark craft steered toward the bright red roof on the waterfront, a beacon for thirsty mariners: Pusser's Outpost.

Standing at the ship's rail, an old one-legged seadog stroked the mangy one-eyed parrot on his shoulder and said to the young man at his side:

"Harken ye, lad. 'Tis a fact that Pusser's supplied strong rum to the British Navy for hundreds of years, starting in 1655. Their grog, 84 proof and called 'Nelson's Blood' by the Jack Tars, was the main reason Britannia ruled the waves. Several snorts o' that stuff, boyo, and ye were ready to take on the world, which is exactly what England did."

"Awesome," said the lad. The old man stared at him, then continued:

"Though the Royal Navy stopped serving tots o' rum in 1970, causing mass desertions, Pusser's kept making their nectar. Ye'll soon see 'tis a smooth yet potent drink, able to make a hairy-chested rogue out of anyone who quaffs it, women included."

"Cool," said the lad. The parrot squawked and tried to bite off the rest of its owner's right ear. The sailor swatted his bird and said:

"Many's the time we pirates would be inside Pusser's for hours, losing all track o' time, taking our pleasure with the fine grog and food. When the tide was right and 'twas time to set sail, the Cap'n had to send his First Mate ashore to roust us out o' there and guide us, stumblin' and singin', back aboard 'ere."

"Gnarly," said the youth.

The grizzled mariner spat: "Ye speaks funny, says I."

"Well, you smell funny. And that ugly parrot of yours has crapped all down the back of your jacket."

The weatherbeaten sailor snorted and stumped off to help make the ship fast to the wharf, muttering about the good old days when disrespectful young twits were flogged.

Soon after, the lice-ridden crew were seated in the cosy confines of Pusser's restaurant, knocking back the first of many Painkillers, a potent drink invented in the BVIs, concocted with two ounces of Pusser's rum and renowned for a smoothness that masked a kick like a Saskatchewan mule.

The waitresses, dark island women with blinding smiles and swift backhands for any who tried to get too friendly, squeezed through the crowd taking food orders. Almost everybody ordered Pusser's other famous product: Caribbean Jerk Pizza, made with jerk pork and/or jerk chicken (and not, though the chef dearly wished otherwise, stupid tourists).

The Painkillers taking effect, the air was soon filled with ribald sea shanties, raucous laughter, outrageous boasts, and strident demands from the waitresses to: "PLEASE, mon, behave yourself, or I fetch de chef an' he have a big knife!"

At last, their buccaneer booty all spent, the motley crew was herded out and poured onto their ship, which cast off and sailed away.

Cleaning up, the Pusser's staff agreed that Canadian tourists can be quite a handful when watching the Stanley Cup playoffs on the bar's satellite TV. Great tippers though. And very polite.

Yar, matey! Your author be scourge of at least two of the seven seas.

"When is the Next Bus?"

"The number you have dialled is incorrect.
Please hang up and try again.
Stupidhead."

Our home is located just outside our city limits. Yet that didn't prevent Ma Bell from giving us a phone number that, except for a single digit, exactly matches the number for our city bus company. In the 25 years we've lived in our house, we've fielded countless wrong numbers intended for the bus depot.

In my darker moments, I'm often sorely tempted to answer these ineptly-dialled, yet innocent, bus enquiries with snarky or inappropriate rejoinders. Something like these:

When is the bus going to arrive? "Never, ma'am. Bus service has been cancelled due to budget cuts. Here's the mayor's number if you want to call and complain." Alternate answer: "Just as soon as the hockey game's over."

Are the buses on time? "Yes sir. If your watch is set to Tokyo time." Alternate answer: a burst of hysterical laughter, then hang up.

I'm just leaving the house. When is the bus arriving at (name of bus stop)? "Right now! RUN! Go, go, GO!" Alternate answer: "Well, we have to wash them all first. They're SO dirty! And then we're going to Turtle Wax them and buff them up so they'll REALLY sparkle! And we're putting EXQUISITE lace doilies along the tops of all the seats, too."

Message on our answering machine: **Why does the bus depot have an answering machine?** If we called her back: "We were all out back going through the bus seats looking for loose change. It's our only means of retirement funding, ma'am." Alternate answer: "We were installing slot machines in all the buses. ATMs too, so bring your debit card."

When is the next bus? "It's ready to go. We were just waiting for you to call. Give me your address and we'll send it right over." Alternate answer: "Just as soon as we finish delivering the rest of the school kids. Watch for a bright yellow bus."

I've been waiting here, like, forever! When's the damn bus coming? "Just as soon as, like, possible. We only have the one damn bus and it has a flat. Like." Alternate answer: "Didn't you hear? This is Health Week. There are no buses running. Everyone's supposed to walk, jog, or bike to work. Chill out and hug a tree, man."

Is this the bus station? "No, ma'am. It's the city morgue. Shall I send someone over to give you an estimate?" Alternate answer: "Naw, it's the Badda Bing strip club. Hey, tell your husband to come in and pay for all his lap dances."

What bus do I take to get to the mall? "I don't know. Please hold while I call the bus station to find out for you." Alternate answer: "This is a call centre in Mumbai. What city are you in, and could you please describe for me the best route to take and the address of your mall and the nearest cross street? Please to speak slowly."

Do the buses run every hour? "When we can get them to run at all." Alternate answer: "Normally, yes. However, our city bus budget is all used up for this month, thanks to the huge increase in our insurance premium because of that horrific accident last year. Regular service will start again the first of next month. In the meantime, we suggest car pooling."

How much is the bus fare from downtown to the zoo? "If you have to ask, you can't afford it." Alternate answer: "Oh, that's much too far for our drivers to go. Ask your neighbour to drive you."

Are the buses still running in this blizzard? "Goodness gracious, no. We're using dog sleds instead. Bundle up real warm, go out to the bus stop, and listen for the barking." Alternate answer: "We lost contact with all of our buses hours ago. We're fearing the worst. Do you know people with snowmobiles? We must rescue the passengers before cannibalism starts."

Hello? Bus station? Wait, is that a party I hear in the background? "Yep. Working here is just one big non-stop party. C'mon down and join us, especially if you're good-looking. Bring beer." Alternate answer: "Yep. That's a clue you dialled the wrong number, Ace."

What time is the first bus tomorrow? "Whaaat? You expect DAILY bus service? Give us a break; we drove all DAY today!" Alternate answer, with sitar music playing softly in the background: "Time? Ah, but what IS time? Is time a natural thing, or is it an artificial construct to keep us enslaved to our corporate masters? In fact, are we even here, or is this all a dream? Strawberry fields forever."

My wife considers it her civic duty not to let me answer the phone.

To Sea or not to Sea?

The debonair secret agent leapt onto the sleek top-of-the-line PWC (personal water craft), releasing the line that tethered it to the dock as he straddled the machine in one fluid movement. As bullets from his pursuers zinged around him, he jammed the weird green-coloured key he had taken from the guard hut into the machine. (He had found three PWC keys of different colours hanging in the unconscious guard's hut. Quickly concluding that green meant "go," he had grabbed that one.) He thumbed the bright red start button.

No sound came from the engine. James muttered a curse and stared at the dashboard's LED screen. "Welcome aboard" it stated.

"Some welcome," James growled.

A bullet zipped past his ear and buried itself into the weathered dock, sending splinters flying. He pulled his Walther from his shoulder holster and returned fire.

BANG! BANG! BANG! Three enemy agents obligingly fell. But there were still at least a dozen more, each firing at him as if their guns had an unlimited supply of ammunition.

He pressed the start button again. There was a single long beep from the dashboard. No sound from the engine. "Welcome aboard" again strolled across the screen.

"Damnation!" said James, turning amidst the hail of bullets and firing his Walther again. BANG! BANG! Two more pursuers crumpled earthward. The rest were getting very close now.

He ripped out the key and reinserted it onto the stem, twisting it left a quarter-turn. He jabbed start. Long beep. He twisted the key a quarter-turn to the right, again hitting start. Long beep.

BANG! BANG! BANG! Three more bad guys fell. A bullet creased James' perfectly-combed hair, ruffling it.

While continuing to return fire, he tried to start the machine *three more times. BANG! Beeeep. BANG! Beeeep. BANG! Beeeep. Then, as enemy bullets bit into the dock, burrowed into the water, and tore deep furrows through the bright yellow skin of the PWC; as James continued to frantically thumb the start button, fearing he'd have to abandon the damn thing and swim for it, taking his chances with the sharks that infested these waters; he suddenly heard two short beeps. The engine started with a roar.*

James yelled triumphantly over his shoulder: "Better luck next time, you incompetent sods!" He mashed the throttle lever hard against the handgrip, expecting the powerful machine to leap forward and leave his enemies far behind in its frothy wake.

The machine trundled ahead at a sedate pace. "What the bloody hell!?" blurted James, as a bullet brushed past his forearm. He stared unbelievingly at the dashboard screen, which read: "Limp Home Mode. Check Engine."

The enemy agents reached the dock. Their gunfire tore into the suave British agent at murderous close range. The multiple impacts knocked him off the PWC and he disappeared beneath the water, which quickly turned red.

"Finally got the bastard!" crowed one swarthy agent. "It's fortunate he never got the one hour training session on how to start these new Sea-Doos."

"Wouldn't have done him any good even if he had," laughed another agent. "The fool stole the Learner key from our guard. Means the machine would only go slow. We'd have caught him easy in our speedboat."

"Oh look: here come the sharks."

* * * * * *

What caused the world's most famous not-so-secret agent to (apparently) die? Glad you asked:

Good friends of ours recently purchased a new, top-of-the-line Sea-Doo personal water craft. Having rented many such chariots during tropical vacations over the years, they eagerly looked forward to similar high-speed fun at their waterfront home:

jumping aboard, straddling the long seat, grabbing the handlebars, inserting the key, hitting the start button, then with a roar of the powerful Rotax engine, jetting off across the lake with whoops of joy.

That was the plan.

In their infinite wisdom, for whatever murky corporate reasons, Bombardier, the makers of Sea-Doo, had engineered a complicated high-tech starting procedure for their latest crop of aquatic rockets. Simple keys were now as passe as good manners. You received three stubby electronic keys, each coloured differently: Learner (slow speed), Rental (where you could program the speed), and I Control (unlimited speed).

To start the beast, you must first "awaken" the on-board computer by pressing the start button. After a message scrolled across the dashboard LED screen, welcoming you aboard, you waited until the screen went blank, then you married your electronic starting "plug" to the electronic "stem" beneath the handlebars and hit the start button again. If, and only if, you were rewarded with two short beeps, then the engine deigned to start. However, if a long beep sounded, then something had not been done properly and the engine would not start. To increase your chances of ignition, you should turn the "plug" key a quarter-turn to the left or right on the "stem." A quick prayer also helped.

The on-board computer was so sophisticated, and so finicky, that if an hapless rider tried too many times to achieve the coveted two short beeps, and failed each time, then the machine went into "Limp Home Mode" and the dreaded "Check Engine" warning flashed on the screen. ("Check Engine" meant you had to haul your water toy all the way back to the dealer, so the repair shop's computer could be hooked up to your PWC's computer, and the two machines could then chortle in binary code at how they had again confounded the puny humans.)

After taking delivery of their Sea-Doo at the start of a long weekend, our friends spent the next three days fruitlessly - and frustratingly - trying to get their persnickety new toy to recognize its new masters and please, please, pretty please, *start*, dammit,

START!

In desperation, they resorted to reading the Owner's Manual. Twice. Same result: dead in the water. They even called in a grizzled mangy Sea-Dog to try and coax their gleaming yellow Sea-Doo into life. I failed.

Come Tuesday, after contacting the dealer in a high state of agitation, a one hour on-site coaching session on how to start their expensive high-tech machine was conducted for them, their children, grandchildren, in-laws, friends, neighbours, pizza delivery boys, and anyone else who might ever conceivably ride the thing.

All of which got my wife thinking: In countless action movies, you often see the hero leap aboard a convenient jet-ski and peel off with bad guys in hot pursuit slinging hot lead. Imagine, she said, if the convenient jet-ski was today's Sea-Doo ...

"Bond? Come in, Bond! Please respond! Hello?"

The Great Big Thing

The Great Big Thing was supposed to save Parsimony. It had *such* potential.

Smothered in dense Northern Ontario forest, connected to the outside world by the thin ribbon of the Trans-Canada Highway and the erratic schedule of Moosehide Airways, with a population of 8,003 (higher during tourist and hunting seasons), the town of Parsimony was dying. Summer tourists and fall hunters notwithstanding, what kept Parsimony's year-round population clothed and fed was the big lumber mill on the shore of Lake Wackawippi at the south end of town. The big lumber mill that closed last month, thanks to the Great Recession and U.S. lumber tariffs.

It wasn't just the unemployed mill workers that devastated the local economy, but the ripple effect of things like unsold groceries at Jerry's IGA, the jeans and plaid shirts gathering dust at Fran's Fine Fashions, and the Jeeps, ATVs and Ski-Doos at Earl's Luxury Rides that now crowded the lot.

The Fates couldn't resist kicking Parsimony when it was down: the Great Recession also crippled tourism nationwide. The town's usually-reliable summer tourist flood dwindled to a trickle.

A pall of gloom stifled Parsimony like chaperones at a teen dance. Folks started moving away, not even bothering to list their homes for sale, because no one wanted them.

Shaken out of its usual lethargy, the Mayor and Council hosted a special Town Hall meeting of the citizenry to develop solutions to the economic crisis. The biggest ballroom at the Black Fly Inn was jammed.

When the Mayor opened the floor to ideas from the audience, bushels of suggestions were made, from relocating a provincial ministry to the town (with hundreds of recession-proof civil service jobs in tow), to building a lavish destination resort (until someone mentioned the spectacular failure of Minaki, near Kenora), to hosting a gigantic dump for Toronto's daily mega-ton garbage harvest (hisses filled the air at the mention of Toronto).

Then fishing guide and ballet instructor Powerful Pierre Laframboise, generally regarded as the town's Idea Man despite never finishing high school, heaved to his feet and said:

"We need to build someting BIG, by Chris'. Someting that no other town 'as. Someting that will bring in *les touristes*, get national media coverage. Someting - "

"That'll get a government grant," interjected His Worship.

"*Oui, exactement.*"

"But there's so many towns that have a big something already," objected Beryl Smythe-Willcocks-McTavish-Jones, manager of the town's sole bank. "Wawa has a big Canada Goose, Dryden has a big moose, Cochrane a big polar bear, Sudbury the Big Nickel. Vulcan, Alberta has the Starship Enterprise, Prince George has the giant Mr. PG log man, Shediac the world's largest lobster. There's even the world's largest fire hydrant and Coke can in Manitoba! The list goes on and on. What would make our big something any different?"

"Because it will be so big, *si unique*, that it will really stand out! The world's biggest, by Chris'!" shouted Powerful Pierre.

"But the world's biggest *what*?" asked Beryl petulantly.

"Marble," came a quiet voice from the back of the room, belonging to Maynard Kooperberg, owner of Koop's Games & Pastries Emporium. "I just Googled it on my Blackberry. No town in North America has one. We should build the world's largest, most colourful marble."

There was a long silence while everyone digested this. Several people looked like they had just swallowed Buckley's Cough Syrup. Then:

"And put it up on a big pedestal!" said Frank Doughty, owner of Frank's Concrete & Fine Gifts.

"And surround it with a beautiful park!" added Betty Johnstone, owner of The Looney Landscaper.

"And sell souvenir t-shirts and ball caps!" said Horace

McDermott, owner of We'll Leave You In Stitches Embroidery and Day Surgery.

"And locate it at the head of main street, so people will pass by our shops and restaurants!" chimed in Susan Straczynski, Chair of the Downtown Business Improvement Association and owner of Susan's Sultry Smorgasbord.

"And tap into the whole nostalgia thing by holding marble tournaments and marble swap meets, so folks will stay overnight!" said Bill Fredricks, owner of the Busy Beaver Bed & Breakfast & Bait.

Enthusiasm swept the room. So, of course, the naysayers had to speak up. Can't have unbridled enthusiasm running rampant. Too dangerous.

The issue was debated far, far into the night. The director of the community cable TV station, which broadcast all Council meetings to a devoted audience of 23, told ribald jokes to his three camerapeople over their headsets, to keep them awake (one fell asleep anyway). As dawn broke, consensus was finally reached: Parsimony would have the World's Biggest Marble.

Matilda Snodgrass, the town's chief administrator, soon discovered that the billions of dollars available under the federal government's new recession-fighting Municipal Infrastructure Program did not apply to the construction of big marbles, no matter how economically-devastated a town was. It just didn't look good, politically.

However, the bureaucrats in Ottawa had not reckoned with Matilda's tenacity and inventiveness. The mayor treated Doris Del Magnifico, their local MP (just returned from a lengthy fact-finding mission to Bora Bora), to drinks at the Field O'Stumps Tavern and Daycare. By closing time, Doris had endorsed Matilda's carefully-crafted submission for a new, state-of-the-art, eco-friendly sewage treatment plant. She was impressed with the plant's unusual large dome and the pretty park that would surround it.

With funding secured, design engineers were hired. The historic 1890 Oswald J. Burnhamthorpe Mansion straddling the head of main street at the north end of town, meant to forever honour the inventor of Donkey Distemper Drops, was expropriated and razed.

The engineers hired the Japanese company that had manufactured the huge two-foot-thick, 120-ton acrylic viewing window for the Georgia Aquarium's whale shark pool, the world's largest, in Atlanta. They would construct the mammoth marble in two halves, ship them to Parsimony, and join the halves together. Instead of being clear, the marble's virtually-indestructible ten-inch-thick acrylic would be embedded with countless swirls of brilliant colours. It would look like an enormous highly-polished agate marble; the ultimate "aggie."

A major hurdle occurred when Council discovered that a host of environmental assessments must first be completed before one shovel could bite dirt. It was, after all, a big sewage treatment plant. Legions of provincial and federal government inspectors descended on Parsimony, armed with thick books of regulations and generous expense accounts. This provided a welcome boost to the town's hospitality industry. Powerful Pierre did a brisk trade as a fishing guide.

Thanks to several evenings at the Field O'Stumps attended by the inspectors and hosted by the tavern's best customer, His Worship, an environmental review process that normally took one year, was completed in two months. Within hours of the requisite permits for a sewage facility being issued, Frank Doughty's crew were erecting forms to pour the concrete for the massive pedestal.

The day the marble arrived in Parsimony was historic. Schools were closed. Shops were shuttered. Speeches were uttered. Everyone lined main street to gawk at the giant half-globes as they slowly passed by, each on separate tractor-trailer flatbeds, shrouded in canvas. The townspeople gasped in unison when the coverings were removed upon arrival at the park. The sunlight hitting the multi-coloured acrylic caused the rainbow swirls to shimmer and sparkle like something alive.

A special crane from Sault Ste. Marie hoisted the acrylic halves onto the thick pedestal. The bottom half went up first, glued to the wide, curved concrete base with the same high-tech glue used to fasten the heat shield tiles to the space shuttle's underbelly (and with the same warranty). Then the top half was seamlessly fused to its mate, using the same technology that had melded together the three massive sections of the sixty-foot-long Georgia Aquarium viewing window.

The completed marble was a ginormous globe dominating the hill down which sloped Parsimony's main street, with the green-and-granite backdrop of the horribly-misnamed Mount Olympus (514 feet high) behind it. Nick-named "Awesome Aggie," the marble was 45 feet in diameter and weighed 4.7 tons. Its smooth, flawless acrylic surface shone with deep iridescent waves of colour.

Parsimony had its Great Big Thing and it was truly marvellous.

The ever-efficient Matilda Snodgrass scheduled the dedication ceremony when Doris Del Magnifico was away on yet another fact-finding mission (this time, to Cannes). Matilda sent media kits to hundreds of national and regional media contacts. No one came, save for a reporter/photographer/advertising/layout person from the *Parsimony Parrot* weekly paper.

Fortunately, Chuck, the 15-year-old son of Maynard Kooperberg, took pictures with his cell phone and posted them on Facebook, MySpace, and YouTube. Tourists started arriving within days.

Within two weeks, the little town was jammed with visitors. Some came to marvel at this feat of engineering, some to recapture marble gaming nostalgia from their youth, others to check off another Big Thing from their Life List, and some to see what $3.2 million taxpayer dollars had purchased.

Parsimony enjoyed an unprecedented tourist boom. Every available guest room was booked. Restaurants were packed. Gift shops crowded to bursting. Other local attractions prospered, like Lumbertown Mini-Golf & Warmish Waterpark.

Six months later, an Ottawa bureaucrat contacted Matilda for photos of the completed sewage plant, "to close the file."

Concealing her nervousness, Matilda asked if someone would be coming to check out the plant.

"Absolutely not," sniffed the bureaucrat. "As our Infrastructure Minister said to the media: 'It's not the federal government's job to track billions of dollars in stimulus funding.' Just send the photos."

Matilda had Chuck take a digital picture, then the teenager Photoshopped the "World's Biggest Marble" sign in the forefront of the scene into "Parsimony Sewage Treatment Plant." On the Internet, Matilda found interior shots of a suitable sewage facility - in Bern, Switzerland - and set those along to Ottawa as well.

Everyone involved in the deception slept soundly. Albeit via a circuitous route, the federal stimulus dollars had done exactly what they were intended to do: revive a moribund town. Not a single tourist would ever have come to see a sewage treatment plant, no matter how state-of-the-art it was. But thousands came to gape at Awesome Aggie.

As the Big Marble's fame grew, so did the tourist flood. Hordes showed up even in winter, traditionally the time when black bears and Parsimonians hibernated. The Black Fly Inn announced a big expansion, prompting its main competitor, the Lusty Lynx Lodge, to follow suit. Then both owners lobbied Council for an injunction to freeze further hotel development, after learning that a new 88-room Travelodge was coming and Super 8 was also interested. Council, salivating for new tax revenue, denied the injunction.

Awesome Aggie drew folks to Parsimony, but once they discovered the area's unspoiled wilderness, they stayed for vacations. The town, recently on death watch, was now flush with year-round business. So one would think all was well.

One would think wrongly.

Parsimonians were woefully unprepared to be smiling, hospitable hosts all year long. Previously, they had months to recover, after the summer tourist and fall hunting seasons ended. Most inhabitants had worked at the lumber mill, without interacting with tourists at all. They weren't trained for this. And, though they were again thankfully employed, hospitality jobs like housekeeping, front desk agent, waiting on tables, and retail clerking paid far less than what the mill had paid, to say nothing of benefits.

Increasing negative comments about surly attitudes and rude behavior posted by visitors on TripAdvisor and similar websites caused great concern at the Chamber of Commerce. Expensive tourism consultants were flown in from "down south" (Southern Ontario, generally regarded as a separate province by Northerners). They ran day-long Customer Service workshops for the townsfolk using the latest buzzwords, positive role-playing exercises, and colourful PowerPoint graphs. The consultants departed with glowing post-workshop evaluations.

It made no difference at all.

Negative reviews from tourists increased. Incidents of domestic violence also increased. After a particularly nasty argument with his wife, Earl ran a snowmobile through his front showroom window. As his terrified wife watched, the enraged manager of the Black Fly Inn punched a hole in their livingroom wall following yet another heated altercation with drunken guests. Sultry Susan brained her husband with an iron fry pan. Dogs became adept at avoiding their masters' kicks. Cats took off.

Awesome Aggie just sat there, a glistening technicolour tourist magnet.

The manager of the Parsimony Airport petitioned Council to lengthen the runway, as Moosehide Airways needed bigger jets to service the increasing demand. Problem: picturesque Mount Olympus blocked the expansion. Council unanimously voted to demolish picturesque Mount Olympus. Problem: solved.

Fortunate Farley Excavating was hired to dispose of Mount Olympus, having expertly done blasting for the Trans-Canada Highway a decade earlier. (Since then, unbeknownst to anyone, Fortunate Farley had discovered alcohol, thanks to a near-fatal blasting accident.)

Farley planned to dismantle the mountain in stages, starting with the summit. The first charges would remove the top, and were carefully placed so the rubble would fall away from the town in front and the airport behind.

With a thunderous boom worthy of Zeus himself, the charges exploded. The summit came clean off, as planned. Thick granite chunks flew everywhere, not as planned. Some crashed into Parsimony's airport terminal and runway. The historic wooden forest fire lookout, built in 1902, became history.

On the other side of now-topless Mount Olympus, boulders rained down on cars and shrieking people, who ran for their lives. Cries of "Damn you, Farley!" punctuated the cacophony. One particularly-large rock hit the Big Marble dead-on.

In a heartbeat, Parsimony's biggest asset became its biggest liability.

Like a gigantic thumb flicking a gigantic aggie, the rock knocked the marble off its pedestal, snapping it free from the space-shuttle glue. The 4.7 ton acrylic leviathan hit the ground, ponderously bounced once, and started to roll, slowly at first, then picking up speed as it went downhill.

Right down main street.

Travelling fast, Awesome Aggie thundered down the street, caroming from side to side like a colossal pinball from hell, crushing everything in its path. It flattened cars and motorcycles, destroyed sidewalk benches and street lamps, and took out the front of every shop and restaurant it hit. (Said restaurants could now offer *al fresco* dining.)

The noise the jumbo juggernaut made as it demolished sounded like Armageddon: horrible loud crunching and cracking sounds, shattering glass, squealing metal, and explosions as squashed automobile gas tanks ignited.

Reaching the end of main street, the behemoth wrecking ball plunged into the cold waters of Lake Wackawippi with a gargantuan splash, plummeting 623 feet to the silty bottom.

Though injuries were numerous, fatalities were avoided because almost everyone had gathered at Big Marble Park to watch Mount Olympus get blasted into mythology.

Parsimony finally achieved national media exposure thanks to its Big Marble. An opportunistic Chuck had filmed *Angry Aggie in*

Action with his cellphone, then uploaded the video to CBC, CTV, and Global, seeking the networks' standing reward for breaking news. Media crews flocked to the half-a-town to cover the disaster. An aerial photo titled "Mashed Main Street" graced the cover of *Maclean's* the following week. A tsunami of tourists arrived to gawk, adding to the townsfolk's misery.

The townsfolk were miserable in more ways than one:

In a final twist worthy of classical Greek tragedy, Awesome Aggie, en route to its watery grave, had trashed Parsimony's 28-year-old sewage treatment plant.

"Human prosperity never rests,
but always craves more,
'till blown up with pride,
it totters and falls."

– Aeschylus, classical Greek
tragic dramatist, 525-456 BC

● ● ● ● ● ● ● ● ●

"You tried your best and failed
miserably. The lesson is:
never try."

– Homer Simpson

About the Author

Since 2003, Bruce Gravel's light-hearted stories have delighted readers of newspapers like the *Peterborough Examiner* and the *Globe & Mail,* and magazines like *Maclean's* and *Association,* among others. His family-friendly wit is suitable for most ages. His first book, *Humour on Wry, with Mustard,* a collection of 88 funny tales, was published in 2008. His second book and first novel, *Inn-Sanity: Diary of an Innkeeper Virgin,* was published in 2009.

Bruce has been President of the Ontario Accommodation Association since 1985, Canada's largest non-profit provincial association specializing in innkeepers, headquartered in Peterborough. He authored the association's widely-used *Innkeeper's Reference Book,* now in its 4th edition.

He lives outside Peterborough, Ontario, with his extremely-tolerant wife, surrounded by rolling farmland that is slowly being devoured by housing developments.

Email him at: bruce@brucegravel.ca

Also available:

INN-SANITY:
DIARY OF AN INNKEEPER VIRGIN
A novel of sex and silliness, tragedy and triumph,
and exploding concrete

Bruce Gravel's well-received novel incorporates hundreds of true-life incidents from actual innkeepers to hilariously, and sometimes poignantly, chronicle the crazy first year of two middle-aged novice innkeepers. Such as: A horse in a motel room! An exploding swimming pool! Giant mutant animals! A Hollywood movie shoot from hell! Saucy walls! A ghost!

For a sample chapter, and to order, visit **www.brucegravel.ca**. Also available at **www.amazon.com**.

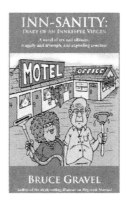

"The book is super. I was thoroughly engaged and had lots of laughs too."

–Colleen Isherwood, Editor, **Canadian Lodging News**

"A great read and very interesting. Wow, hard to believe the stories are based on real events!"

– Kim Litchfield, Corporate Account Manager, WSPS

Also available:

HUMOUR ON WRY, WITH MUSTARD
88 Tasty Treats to Feed Your Funny-bone

Bruce Gravel's wonderful book of short stories, that is guaranteed to cause smiles, chuckles, snorts, guffaws, and even some belly-laughs, with funny tales of everyday life. (There are cartoons too!)

Don't take our word for it! For the entire first chapter, and to order, visit **www.brucegravel.ca**. Also available at **www.amazon.com**.

"The story about eating dessert first cracked me right up!"
– Colleen Isherwood, Editor, ***Canadian Lodging News***

"I would like to complain about that 'I, Robot' story. It caused me to pull a muscle in my cheek from laughing so hard."
– Letter to the Editor of the ***Globe & Mail***